MOTORCYCLE ARIZONA!

A guide to touring Arizona by motorcycle

by

Frank Del Monte

GOLDEN WEST ☼ PUBLISHERS

Cover photo by Dennis Scully

— DISCLAIMER —

I have tried very hard to make everything in this book as accurate as possible. The miles in the day rides are darn good. The hours are subjective. The attractions described are as I remember them and you must accept the descriptions as being my opinion. The same goes for the accommodations. Things change rapidly nowadays. The publisher as well as myself may not be held responsible for lost time, money, injury, or damages incurred as a result of using this book. However, if you find any errors, please let us know!   —Frank Del Monte

---

Library of Congress Cataloging-in-Publication Data
Del Monte, Frank
Motorcycle Arizona! / by Frank Del Monte.
        p.   cm.
1. Motorcycling—Arizona—Guidebooks.   2. Arizona—Description and travel.   I. Title.
GV1059.522.A6D45   1994   94-38135
796.7'5'09791—dc20   CIP

ISBN #0-914846-99-X

Printed in the United States of America.

Golden West Publishers, Inc.
4113 N. Longview
Phoenix, AZ 85014 USA
(602) 265-4392

Dedication

This book is dedicated to all the Western States Motorcycle Tours and Rentals clients, past, present, and future, for wanting to know, "Where to go, what to see, where to stay."

This book is especially dedicated to Jeremy Lindsay (England) and Annette Jensen (Denmark), our very first guided tour victims ..err... clients.

Revision Notes

This is the second version of this book and includes easier to read typeface, updated maps, new rides, more accommodation listings, and a whole passel of other good stuff.

Acknowledgements

I wish to thank the Chambers of Commerce and Visitor Information Centers in the following towns and states for the reams of information they provided: Arizona State, Apache Junction, Benson, Bisbee, Bowie, Colorado State, Douglas, Flagstaff, Globe/Miami, Graham County, Greenlee County, Lake Havasu City, Nevada, Phoenix, Scottsdale, Show Low, Sierra Vista, Tombstone, Utah State, Willcox, Williams, and Yuma.

I also wish to thank Mr. Gus Walker for the beautiful Arizona State and Day Ride Maps he created. Those maps really help make this book usable.

And last, but certainly not least, I thank my ever loving wife for writing the foreword to this book, and for "editing my words, so the prose flows." (She didn't see that last sentence.)

Foreword

by Cheryl Thomas

"My heroes have always been cowboys"... so goes the song, and so goes my fascination with people who ride motorcycles. Imagine the movie scene where the cowboy sweeps past a woman dressed in fringed leather, scoops her up behind him on his horse and gallops off into the sunset. That's the thrill I'm talking about.

When I dress for motorcycling I could just as well be heading for the stables as for the garage. Let's see, jeans, leather high top boots, heavy jacket, and don't forget the bandanna. Cowgirl, right? Trade the Stetson for a helmet and I'm all set.

Our life in the Southwest helps complete the image for me. When I throw my leg over the pillion and Frank makes the bike surge into a sweeping turn, I know I'm heading for Saguaro-filled desert or pine-covered mountains. Looking across the landscape it's easy to see the image of horse and rider keeping pace in the shimmering heat waves rising from the desert floor. He's a ghost from the past riding across the range and into the sunset. The shadow of the bike distorts on the pavement, and in my imagination we are cowboy and cowgirl...wide brimmed hats, gun belts strapped on, and a trusty Winchester slung across the saddle.

The clouds shift and we are again on two wheels, purring down the mountain with the engine turned off, coasting silently through the twists and turns, down, down, down, into the valley below. As I watch a hawk circling aimlessly above us and the sun casting a red blaze behind the mountain, visions of life on the range pull me in time after time. Soon the Saguaros are replaced by towering pines as the bike climbs north on tranquil back roads away from crowded cities and freeways.

It doesn't take much imagination to see this country as it was when everyone living here was a cowboy or cowgirl. It is still hard to fathom, though, how pioneers in wagon trains made their laborious journeys through land as rugged as this. What kept them going? Was it the search for independence from a crowded world and the miles and miles of open range and freedom calling them?

When you tour our state of Arizona, be conscious of your shadow along the road. If it should cast an image of wide-brimmed riders astride gallant steeds, let your mind ride with them far across the deserts, over Saguaro-covered mountains into box canyons with hidden caves and gold mines.

Table of Contents

**Ribbons of highway wind through cactus-filled deserts
as well as pine-covered mountains.**

(Photo by Vince Maietta)

Arizona roads provide beautiful vistas, spectacular scenery and the opportunity to enjoy peaceful solitude.

(Photo by author)

How this Book is Organized.

In writing this book I've tried to follow the KISS principle (Keep It Simple Stupid). I figure you're interested in five things, how to tour, where to tour, how to get there, what to see, and where to stay.

Section 1:　General hints and helpful information.

Section 2:　Suggested one and two week tours made of town to town day rides. The towns I chose to ride to and from are:

> **Arizona:**
> | | |
> |---|---|
> | Bisbee | Phoenix |
> | Chinle (Canyon de Chelly) | Sedona |
> | Eagar | Show Low |
> | Flagstaff | Tucson |
> | Grand Canyon South Rim | Willcox |
> | Grand Canyon North Rim | Williams |
> | Lake Havasu City | Yuma |
>
> **Colorado:**
> | | |
> |---|---|
> | Cortez | Durango |
>
> **Nevada:**
> | | |
> |---|---|
> | Boulder City | Las Vegas |
>
> **Utah:**
> Mexican Hat

Section 3:　Descriptions of day rides from a starting town to a destination town. These are the rides which when combined form the suggested one and two week tours in section one. The routes were chosen to give you the most scenic ride on roads most attractive to motorcyclists.

Section 4:　Descriptions of the attractions located in and around the destination towns and cities.

Section 5:　Listings of accommodations in the day ride and tour towns.

Helpful Information and General Touring Hints.

Important Telephone Numbers.

Police/Fire/Emergency	All Arizona	911
Police	Phoenix	602-262-6151
Police	Tucson	602-791-4452
Police - AZ Highway Patrol	All Arizona	800-525-5555
		602-223-2000
Road Conditions	Central AZ	602-729-2000
		Press "ROAD"
Road Conditions	Southern AZ	602-292-1000
		Press "ROAD"
Road Conditions	Eastern AZ	602-537-7623
		602-368-8841
Doctor Referral	Phoenix	602-252-2844
24 Hour Medical Emergency	Phoenix	602-234-0026
24 Hour Medical Emergency	Scottsdale	602-990-2044
24 Hour Pharmacy	Phoenix	602-247-1014
24 Hour Pharmacy	Scottsdale	602-481-4444
Passport Information		602-262-1156
Foreign Currency Exchange	Phoenix	602-468-1199
Foreign Currency Exchange	Scottsdale	602-949-7000
Lost Travelers Checks	AMEX	800-221-7282
Lost Travelers Checks	BankAmerica	800-227-3460
Lost Travelers Checks	VISA	800-227-6811
Cables/Telegrams		800-325-6000

Historic Trains.

Cottonwood Train	602-639-0010
Williams Steam Train to the Grand Canyon	800-843-8724
Durango/Silverton Steam Train (Colorado)	303-247-2733

Major Airlines.

Alaska Airlines	800-426-0333
Alitalia	800-221-4745
American	800-433-7300
America West	800-235-9292
British Airways	800-247-9297
Continental	800-231-3181
Delta	800-221-1212
Morris Air	800-466-7747
Midwest Express	800-452-2022
Northwest	800-225-2525
Lufthansa	800-645-3880
Qantas	800-227-0290
Southwest	800-453-9417
Swissair	800-221-4750
TWA	800-892-2746
United	800-241-6522
USAir	800-428-4322

Historic Hotels and Bed & Breakfasts.

Historic Hotels of the Rocky Mountains	800-626-4886
Arizona Association of B&B Inns	602-231-6777
Bed and Breakfast in Arizona	800-266-7829
Mi Casa Su Casa B&B Service	800-456-0682
Old Pueblo Home Stays	800-333-9776

Major Hotel Chains.

Best Western	800-528-1234
Clarion, Rodeway, Comfort Inn	800-424-6423
Days Inn	800-329-7466
Doubletree Hotels	800-222-8733
Embassy Suites	800-362-2779
Hampton Inns	800-426-7866
Hilton	800-445-8667
Howard Johnson	800-654-2000
Holiday Inns	800-465-4329
Marriott Courtyard	800-321-2211
Marriott Fairfield	800-228-2800
Marriott Hotels	800-228-9290

Quality Inns	800-221-2222
Quality Suites	800-228-5151
Ramada Hotels	800-272-6232
Red Lion	800-547-8010
Residence Inn	800-331-3131
Sheraton	800-325-3535
Travelodge	800-578-7878
Westin Hotels	800-228-3000
Windmill Inns	800-547-4747

Visitor Information Organizations.

Arizona (State)	800-842-8257
California (State)	800-862-2543
Colorado (State)	800-433-2656
Nevada (State)	800-638-2328
New Mexico (State)	800-545-2040
Texas (State)	800-888-8839
Utah (State)	801-538-1030
Alpine COC	602-339-4330
Apache Junction	602-982-3141
Benson	602-586-2842
Bisbee	602-432-2141
Bowie	602-847-2448
Clifton COC	602-865-3313
Cottonwood COC	602-634-7593
Douglas	602-364-2477
Eagar	602-333-2123
Flagstaff	800-842-7293
Globe/Miami	602-425-4495
Graham County	602-428-2511
Greenlee County	602-865-3313
Kingman	602-753-6106
Lake Havasu City	602-453-3444
Las Vegas, NV COC	702-735-1616
Las Vegas, NV (Marriage Info)	702-455-3156
Phoenix - Visitor Information	800-528-0483
Phoenix COC	602-254-5521
Pinetop/Lakeside	602-367-4290
Scottsdale	602-945-8481
Sierra Vista	602-458-6940
Silverton, CO COC	800-752-4494

Show Low	602-537-2326
Snowflake/Taylor	602-536-4331
Springerville/Eagar	602-333-2123
Strawberry	602-476-3547
St. Johns	602-337-2000
Tombstone	602-457-2211
Tubac COC	602-398-2704
Tucson	602-624-1817
Willcox	602-384-2272
Yuma COC	602-782-2567

Ghost Towns.

There are hundreds of ghost towns in Arizona. Far too many to list here. Most of them are on back country dirt roads not suitable for touring motorcycles. Believe me, I am not kidding! The easiest to reach on paved roads are: **Oatman** in the Northwest, **Jerome** in the North/Central, and **Dos Cabezas** in the Southeast parts of the state. See their descriptions in the back of this book.

Indian Reservations.

There are 14 Native American Tribes residing in Arizona on 20 reservations. These reservations are considered to be separate nations. Arizona law takes precedence on the main roads through the reservations but tribal law applies once you are off the main roads. Each tribe has its own unique lifestyle and heritage. Feel free to visit the reservations, but please respect the residents' rights and customs. Remember, you are visiting their homes! They live here. Don't take pictures without asking permission. Don't trespass on posted land. Tribal permits are required for camping, fishing, or hunting.

General Information.

AZ Commission of Indian Affairs	602-255-3123
AZ Office of Tourism	602-542-8687

Specific Reservation Information.

Ak-Chin	Central	602-568-2227
Camp Verde	North	602-567-3649
Cocopah East & West	West	602-627-2102
Colorado River	West	602-669-9211
Fort Apache	Northeast	602-338-4346
Fort McDowell	Central	602-990-0995
Fort Mojave	Northwest	602-326-4591
Fort Yuma	West	602-572-0213
Gila River	Central	602-963-4323
Havasupai	Northwest	602-448-2961
Hopi	Northeast	602-734-2441
Hualapai	Northwest	602-769-2216
Kaibab-Paiute	North	602-643-7245
Navajo	Northeast	602-871-4941
Tohono O'Odham (Papago)	South	602-383-2221
Pascua-Yaqui	Southwest	602-883-2838
Salt River	Northeast	602-941-7277
San Carlos	Northeast	602-475-2361
Tonto-Apache	Northeast	602-474-5000
Yavapai-Prescott	Northwest	602-445-8790

Arizona Weather.

"If you don't like the weather,
ride an hour and find some you do like."

Arizona ranges from low deserts to tall mountains and everything in between. Because of these altitude changes the weather differences around the state can be impressive. It is not unusual for Arizona to have both the highest and lowest national temperatures on the same day!

I once rode a circle route from Phoenix (100 degrees) to Payson (rain), Happy Jack (hail), Flagstaff (snow), Sedona (hail), Prescott (rain), Wickenburg (sunny), and returned to Phoenix (100 degrees) all in one day.

Another time I was sitting at a stop light in Phoenix and I noticed the car next to me had snow skis on its roof rack, and the car in front of them was towing a boat loaded with water skis. So, no matter what your sport, there's weather available to enjoy. The charts below will give you an idea of the average high and low temperatures around the state.

Average High Temperatures

	Jan	Feb	Mar	Apr	May	Jun	Jul	Aug	Sep	Oct	Nov	Dec
Flagstaff	42	49	53	59	68	79	84	78	73	70	51	43
Grand Canyon	41	45	50	60	70	76	85	91	78	65	52	43
Lake Havasu	67	72	78	87	95	103	108	106	102	91	77	68
Phoenix	65	75	79	85	94	106	107	104	98	94	75	68
Show Low	44	48	53	63	73	82	85	85	79	68	55	45
Tucson	67	73	77	83	93	104	101	98	94	89	74	65
Winslow	44	55	61	68	78	88	93	87	82	77	59	49
Yuma	68	74	78	86	94	100	106	105	102	91	78	69

Average Low Temperatures

	Jan	Feb	Mar	Apr	May	Jun	Jul	Aug	Sep	Oct	Nov	Dec
Flagstaff	21	24	35	33	46	55	66	58	54	51	34	22
Grand Canyon	23	25	30	40	50	56	65	71	58	45	32	23
Lake Havasu	47	52	58	67	75	83	88	86	82	71	51	40
Phoenix	45	55	59	65	74	86	87	84	78	74	55	48
Show Low	17	21	25	32	38	47	55	54	47	35	24	19
Tucson	47	53	57	63	73	84	81	78	74	69	54	45
Winslow	24	35	41	68	58	68	73	67	62	57	39	29
Yuma	36	39	44	50	57	63	73	74	66	54	44	38

Talking Arizona.

You'll run into a lot of strange words and place names in our state. Part of the influence is due to our Native American culture and part is due to the early Spanish explorers. Here are some words to watch for:

Agua Fria	A-wha-fre-a	"Cold Water".
Ajo	Ah-ho	An Arizona city.
Canyon de Chelly	Canyon-d'-Shay	A National Monument.
Casa Grande	Ca-sa Grand-ay	"Big House".
Cholla	Choy-ya	A cactus.
Fajitas	Fa-heet-as	A good Mexican food.
Gila Bend	Heela Bend	An Arizona city.
Gila Monster	Heela Monster	A large poisonous lizard.
Hopi	Ho-pee	Native American Tribe.
Jalapeno	Holl-a-peen-ya	A hot chile pepper.
Javelina	Have-a-leen-a	A wild (and very mean) pig.
Mogollon Rim	Mogy-yon Rim	A 300 mile long cliff.
Navajo	Nav-a-ho	Native American Tribe.
Ocotillo	O-ko-tee-yo	A cactus.
Pima	Pee-ma	Native American Tribe.
Pinon	Peen-yon	A type of pine tree.
Saguaro	Soo-war-oh	A large cactus.
Taco	Tah-ko	A good Mexican food.
Tempe	Temp-ee	An Arizona city.
Tortilla	Tor-tee-ya	A flat, round bread.
Tucson	Too-son	An Arizona city.

Arizona Eating.

Arizona offers every kind of food imaginable, but we're really known for our Mexican restaurants. Try some Mexican food while you're here. It's great!

One special note to our foreign visitors. "Chicken Fried Steak" is an American dish, and is a breaded and fried ground beef patty. There's no chicken in it. I pass that bit of information on in remembrance of a young lad from London, who after finishing a goodly portion, remarked, "This is the strangest chicken I've ever eaten."   Also, just in case you've ever wondered, "Rocky Mountain Oysters" **do not** come from the ocean. They come from sheep. Don't ask.

Arizona Must See List.

People are always asking me what I would try to see if I were visiting and only had limited time. So here's my own "must see" list for Arizona. Unless you have a month or more to spend on the road, **there is no way you can see all these sights in a single vacation.** This means you get to come back!

Central
The Florence Museum.

Casa Grande Indian Ruins.

North
Wickenburg.
The Grand Canyon - IMAX Theater.
The Grand Canyon - South Rim.
The Grand Canyon - 26 Mile Scenic Drive.

Tuzigoot Indian Ruins.
Sedona.
Jerome.
Prescott.

North/East
Canyon De Chelly.
Four Corners.

Monument Valley.
Hubbell Trading Post.

North/West
Oatman.

South
Tucson - Sonoran Desert Museum.
Tucson - Mission San Xavier del Bac.
Tucson - The Titan Missile Silo.

Tucson - Pima Air Museum.
Tucson - Old Tucson.

South/East
The Chiricahuas.
Dragoon - The Amerind Foundation.
Bisbee - The Copper Queen Mine Tour.

The Dos Cabezas Cemetery.
Tombstone.

East
The Salt River Canyon.
The Coronado Trail.

The Petrified Forest.

West
Lake Havasu - London Bridge.
Quartsite - Hi Jolly Gravesite.

Yuma - Territorial Prison.

Arizona Trivia.

Arizona has four nicknames:

"The Grand Canyon State" because it contains the Grand Canyon.
"The Copper State" because of its huge copper deposits.
"The Valentine State" because it was made a state on Valentine's Day,
February 14, 1912.
"The Baby State" because it was the last of the original 48 states.

The State Seal includes figures representing the three big C's. Copper, Cattle, and Cotton. The miner in the seal was a real person as his figure was taken from an old photograph.

The State Motto is "Ditat Deus", meaning God Enriches.

The State Flag includes a copper colored star (not gold, not yellow). The blue field represents honor. The red and gold represent the Arizona sun.

The State Colors are Blue and Gold.

The State Song is "Arizona" by Margaret Rowe, although a strong alternative (and better known) is another "Arizona" by Rex Allen Jr.

The State Flower is the Saguaro Cactus Blossom.
The State Tree is the Paloverde.
The State Bird is the Cactus Wren. (Not the Roadrunner!)
The State Necktie is the Bola Tie (String Tie), which originated in Arizona.
The State Vehicle is the Motorcycle. (Not true. I made that up.)
The State Gem is Turquoise.
The State Dance is the Square Dance.
The State Amphibian is the Tree Frog.
The State Fish is the Apache Trout.

Arizona is considered to be a desert state and yet it has 75 lakes. Only one of those lakes (Montezuma's Well) is natural. The other 74 are man-made.

Arizona has more power and sail boats per capita than any other state!

Arizona has seven National Forests. The Apache, Coconino, Coronado, Kaibab, Prescott, Tonto, and Sitgreaves.

Arizona has three pyramid shaped grave/monuments.

- The first is the grave of "The Father of Arizona", Charles Debrille Poston, and is located on Poston's Butte just north of the town of Florence.
- The second is the grave of our first governor, George W. P. Hunt, and is located in Papago Park in Phoenix.
- The third is the grave of Hi Jolly, an Arabian camel driver. It is located in Quartzsite.

Kachina Dolls.

The original kachina dolls were representations of the Hopi Spirit Dancers that are integral to the Hopi religion. The dolls represent the Spirit Dancers in full costume. True Hopi dolls are hand carved from cottonwood tree root that has been dead for 10 to 15 years. The complete dolls are usually carved from several pieces of wood. Even the costume, feathers, shells, bows are carved. Some Hopi carvers are so skilled that their dolls are carved from a single piece of wood. Of course, these kachinas are very rare and expensive.

Kachinas became popular in the 1960's when they were "discovered" by personalities such as John Wayne, Charlton Heston, Clint Eastwood, and Barry Goldwater. Because of the demand, and because carving true Hopi kachinas takes a long time, a second source became available. The Navajo kachina.

Navajo kachinas are not authentic representations of Hopi Spirit Dancers. However, they allow more people to own kachinas at much more reasonable cost. Navajo kachinas use leather, feathers, string, yarn, bells and other decorations. They are also much brighter than Hopi kachinas. Navajo kachinas are very affordable and make great souvenirs and gifts. They are a fine way to take a piece of Arizona home with you.

Saguaro Cactus.

Saguaro (Soo-war-oh) Cactus grow only in a few areas in the USA because of the very specific conditions they require to survive. Arizona and New Mexico are the only areas I know which can support these desert monoliths. Watch as you ride from low desert where the Saguaro thrive, to the higher elevations of the state. The Saguaro will disappear abruptly! One minute they're everywhere, the next minute there's not one to be seen.

Saguaro usually live to be 150 to 200 years old but there are much older ones still hanging around. The first arms appear at about age 75 after a year of heavy rains. They first bloom (the bloom is the Arizona State Flower) when they are between 35 and 50 years old. These giant cactus weigh up to 3 tons and consist mostly of water! However, please don't cut into a cactus looking for a drink. It doesn't work, it hurts the cactus, and you might get arrested as they are protected by law.

If you see a "pinched" area around the body of a Saguaro it marks how tall the Saguaro was when a hard freeze hit the area. The top froze, died, and the new growth pushed its way through the dead tissue. The Saguaro body will grow arms, and the arms will grow arms. That indicates a very old Saguaro! It's been my observation that the second arms will not grow until the first arms are as tall as the body was when the first arms sprouted.

Gila woodpeckers and flickers bore nesting holes in the cactus. Starlings, purple martin, and small owls use the nesting holes after the woodpeckers move out. To protect itself, the cactus lines the holes with a secretion which forms a hard shell. After the cactus dies these hard shells can be found in the decaying body. They look really weird. There are some on display at the Casa Grande Ruins in Coolidge. Hawks love to sit on the top of Saguaro and watch for ground prey, so watch the tops of the Saguaro as you ride by.

Hazardous Arizona.

Arizona is a great state for motorcycling. Clear skies, warm weather, and great roads. On the other hand, be on the lookout for such hazards as;

Tar Snakes: These are the squiggly black lines you'll see all over the roads. The highway department fills cracks in the road surface with hot tar to keep out water. In hot weather the tar snakes get soft and your wheels tend to slip sideways a few inches in hard turns. This can be most disconcerting!

Slopey Shoulders: The edges (shoulders) of the roads tend to be graded for rain drainage so they slope down and away from edge of the hard surface. The shoulders are also usually dirt and gravel. So when you pull off onto the shoulder and go to put your right foot down, you'll find it won't reach! When it finally does contact the ground it's in loose gravel. This makes for a lot of fall overs to the right. I see it all the time.

No Guard Rails: Arizona and other western states allow you to ride off the sides of mountains if you want to. Consider not doing that. It can really hurt. Slow down on mountain roads! If you go blasting into a turn the next stop could be several hundred feet straight down.

Oily Roads: Because Arizona doesn't get a lot of rain, oil tends to collect at street intersections. Be careful when coming to a stop. Don't depend on your front brake only. For the same reason, be careful when riding in a gentle rain. The oil on the roads floats on the water and makes the road very slick until enough rain has fallen to wash away the oil.

Soft Asphalt: The hot Arizona sun can soften the asphalt in parking lots. Be careful when parking. The side stand, and even the center stand can dig into the soft surface and allow the bike to fall over.

Sand in the Curves: Sand tends to collect in the corners of curvy mountain roads. So just about the time you're really enjoying yourself your traction goes away. This can ruin your whole day. Or life. Be careful!

Oil and Dirt: For some unknown reason, Arizona cities will sometimes resurface a road with a mixture of light oil and dirt. This makes a slippery, gooey mess which will kill motorcyclists in a second. I guess they don't think about us when they make these decisions. Dumb!

Tire Treads: The hot Arizona temperatures are really tough on big truck tires. Especially the recapped ones. If you see pieces of tire tread in the road, slow down! The rest of the tread is ahead of you and if you run into it it can wreck you in an instant.

Off Road/Dirt Road: Unless you are on a dual purpose bike stay on hard surface roads. Going off road is just not worth the danger. Hard packed roads can turn to sand and bury your tires up to the axel and you will be stuck for good. You might die. I am not kidding. We lose several tourists every year out here because of dumb desert driving.

Animals: As you ride, watch for...hawks, soaring overhead, or sitting on the very top of cactus and telephone poles. Eagles in the high country, roadrunners and desert rats everywhere. You may also see buzzards, squirrels, lizards, snakes, coyotes, deer, antelope, lynx, javalinas, mountain lions, and bears. And all that from the seat of your bike!

Be careful at night. Watch for deer, elk, coyotes, horses, and cattle on the roads. They are always just where you don't expect them. Hitting any one of them can be fatal. I'm serious. Slow down at night.

Be considerate of people on horses. Swing wide and give them plenty of room so you don't spook the horses. Be nice. If you run across Navajo herding sheep please slow down or stop. They have the right of way.

Sun Protection: I always wear gloves and a long sleeve shirt or jacket when I ride, even in the hot summertime. I feel more comfortable this way as I really don't like to cover my arms and hands with sun screen lotion. However, since I ride with an open face helmet I do use sun screen on my face. I recommend a sun screen of at least SPF of 35. My wife is fair skinned and she uses SPF 45! SPF 10 won't help you at all. We 'Zonies wear that stuff at night!

Dehydration: Be sure to carry a bottle of water with you in the summer between May and August. I usually fill a large plastic soft drink bottle with water and freeze it over night. Then I wrap it in a towel and it stays cold for 24 hours. Drink lots of water with your meals, and between meals. Dehydration is sneaky and can slip up on you very quietly. You'll find yourself doing stupid things and wondering why. Be careful! Drink lots of liquids but stay away from beer and other alcoholic drinks. They don't help, they hinder. Avoid soft drinks also. Drink water! Don't worry about what the fish do in it!

Pack Light, Right, Tight.

Before riding off on your grand Arizona adventure, let's review a few basic, and hopefully helpful hints concerning picking and packing your luggage.

Packing Light.

The key to packing light is in choosing your "goes withs" and "stays homes". The best way to do this is to set up two categories, one for items you **know** you'll need and absolutely have to have with you, and another for everything else. Then leave home all the "everything else". In other words, if you don't **know** you'll need it, leave it home. If you don't know the day, hour, and minute you're going to need it, leave it home! Don't get trapped by the "I might need this" syndrome. Please read this paragraph twice. <u>Now read it twice again.</u>

Now reality. Pack light, yes, but don't leave out anything that's really important to you. For example, I always take along my hot water bottle! I know on every tour, sooner or later, I'm going to end the day with a screaming headache and a hot water bottle on the back of my neck sure makes my life easier.

There are two very important rules to remember when choosing your clothing. The first is, no matter how long your tour, pack only enough clothes for one week. No more. Think about it. **There is no sense in riding around the second week of your tour with a week's dirty laundry in your saddle bags!** So if your tour is longer than a week stop and do laundry or have it done for you. My wife and I like the second option. We have our laundry done while we take a local area day ride.

The second rule is, leave your fancy clothes at home. The Southwest is a very informal region, so dress up clothes just aren't needed. Ladies don't need dresses or skirts, and guys don't need jackets or ties, as slacks, blue jeans, sport shirts, and boots are acceptable everywhere, even the most expensive restaurants.

Just for the record, I carry (in addition to what I leave home wearing):

> 1 Pair of blue jeans
> 6 Long sleeve, turtle neck (tall neck) shirts (Fall/Winter), or
> 6 Short sleeve, T shirts (Spring/Summer)
> 6 Pair of socks
> 6 Pair of underwear

1 Pair swim trunks or shorts
1 Lightweight wind breaker jacket
1 Down-filled ski jacket (All year)
1 Gloves, light weight
1 Gloves, heavy weight
1 Rain suit with lightweight rubber boots (Important!)
1 Hat with a brim (baseball cap)

Packing Right.

The biggest obstacle to packing light seems to be our morning necessities. The best way to cut down on the bulk is to plan ahead, and DON'T PACK THE ONES YOU USE AT HOME.

Purchase small bottles of shampoo, shaving cream, and deodorant. Two or three ounces of each will carry you through two weeks very nicely. If you run short there are plenty of places to buy more. If you want to use the brand you're used to, purchase some small bottles from the back packing section of a sporting goods store and fill them yourself. I keep a travel kit in a nylon bag which measures 5" by 7" by 1" and contains:

One full size toothbrush.
Two 1 oz. bottles of shampoo.
One 1 oz. bottle of hand cream.
One 1.4 oz tube of toothpaste.
One tube of lip balm.
Two plastic razors.
One package of dental floss.
One small bar of soap.
One small package of aspirin.
Tweezers.
Ten Band-Aids.

I also pack a small can (6 oz.) of shaving cream, the smallest can of deodorant I can find, and a very small (almost pocket size) 1200 watt hair dryer. **Please, leave that huge, 10 pound, industrial strength hair drier at home!** My wife and I share most of the above, but she also carries her feminine stuff, jewelry, hairbrush, and make up. By the way, in order to avoid soggy clothes, pack all liquid items inside plastic zipper lock bags. Changes in altitude tends to make bottles leak.

Packing Tight.

Now that you've chosen your "goes withs", let's talk about packing them down real tight. Space is limited, so the objective is to use it effectively.

The first rule is; forget about folding your clothes, roll them instead. Rolled clothes take less room and give you more options for using the nooks and crannies in your luggage or saddle bags. Folded clothes present a mental road block as square clothes seem to have to go into square corners.

Pack hard objects such as deodorant and shaving cream cans along the top, bottom, and ends of your bags. Save the middle for squeezables and breakables such as hair dryers and curling irons. Load the bags evenly and keep the heavy items to the bottom. Keep the bag weights about the same.

Pack your bike cover in a stuff sack and put it on the luggage rack. A second stuff sack can be used for jackets, gloves, and other items you may want easy access to while on the road.

One last hint in case you are flying out west to pick up a rental bike. When you pack your bags for the air flight, put some of your and your companion's clothing in each bag. If one bag should get lost, you'll at least have some clothes for each of you.

Cameras and Video Equipment.

I spent years lugging a 35MM SLR camera around. I had wide angle, telephoto, and macro lenses, a tripod, and all the other gizmos and gadgets needed for serious photo making. At the same time my wife carried her 35MM pocket camera. When we compared pictures she would usually have as many "keepers" as I did.

Now I carry a shirt-pocket camera. It has auto-everything and I love it. So, in the interest of packing light, consider a pocket camera. Spend your time enjoying the Southwest rather than trying to take it home with you.

I don't own a video camera, but I've had several friends and clients who have packed them along. Usually the results are less than great. The Southwest is HUGE, WIDE, EXTREMELY LARGE COUNTRY. It doesn't fit into the lens of a video camera. In order to record anything you have to do a lot of panning and even that doesn't capture the magnitude. It's like trying to watch a football game through a straw.

Taking video from the back seat doesn't seem to work very well. Too much bouncing, and all you see is the road directly ahead. The opinion so far is video cameras and motorcycles don't (yet) mix. However, if you happen to have an extremely small eight millimeter video camera with a very wide angle lens and auto-stabilization . . . Heck, bring it along. It might work great.

Keeping Yours What is Yours.

Leave your expensive jewelry at home. Wear a cheaper watch. There is no sense to losing or damaging the good stuff. Buy a money belt and keep your extra cash out of sight. Wear one of those belt sacks if you can stand them. I can't.

Don't carry your wallet in your back pocket. Put it into a front pocket, or inside pocket in your jacket. I have a leather pouch that mounts on my bike's tank with hook and loop patches. I snap it off and carry it with me on a short strap under my armpit. I keep my wallet, keys, change, and other stuff in there and ride with empty pockets. It works for me.

Don't leave stuff laying loose on the bike. Use a helmet lock if you're going to leave your helmets behind. Always lock the saddle bags. If your bike doesn't have an alarm system, consider buying one. I really like the "Gorilla" alarm (Gorilla Products - 800-262-6267). For $49.95 it can't be beat. It is so small it fits on any bike nicely. It uses a miniature transmitter for setting and clearing and is very sensitive to the bike being touched. It even has a warn away feature.

Personal Security.

Guns. You don't need them. Leave them home. Yes, this is the wild west, and yes, it is still wild. But it's not that wild and you don't need to fear for your safety or belongings. It is legal to carry firearms in Arizona as long as you keep them in plain view, such as in a holster. However, that same holstered gun will deny you admission to a lot of places. The law says you may carry a gun, but business owners have the right to say you can't enter their establishments doing so. Also, it is illegal to take a gun into a National Park. Don't do it!

There is also the question of the gun being a "concealed weapon" if you have it in the saddle bag or tour pack. The bottom line is you don't need the hassles you might run into. Leave them home.

Daily Riding Hours.

Slow down and smell the cactus!

I've had hundreds of clients return from tour and I've asked them, "Did you see...

The Tuzigoot ruins?	No, no time.
The IMAX theater?	No.
The big old engines at Jerome?	No, no time.
The cowboy bar behind Mormon Lake?	No.
Frog Rock?	No.
Hermit's Roost at the Grand Canyon?	No.
The Amerind Foundation in Dragoon?	No, no time.
The Copper Queen Mine?	No.
The Titan Missile Silo?	No.

"What did you see? " "We saw 4200 miles in seven days."

Folks, that's no way to tour! For goodness sakes, slow down! This is a vacation! The Southwest is big country and you can't "do" it all in a week. Or two weeks. Or even 15 years. I know, I've been trying. So slow down, plan less, enjoy more, and in order to have some fun on your tour, figure:

You will average 200 miles each day.
You will average 40 miles per hour.
You really should spend two days at the Grand Canyon.

The average speed is not as low as you might think, and the miles are not as few as you think. I know you can do more. I know you have done more. I know you are a bigger, better, badder, tougher, faster rider than I am, but I also know that even you have to slow down in small towns, buy gas and meals, make potty stops, and possibly even take an occasional photograph. You may average a bit better than 40 mph, but it won't be much.

So figure on being in the saddle 5 hours each day. If you add to that 3 to 5 hours of actually seeing the sights you're riding through, you'll come up with an 8 to 10 hour day. So, be on the road at 8 AM, ride until 6 PM, **and relax and have some fun!**

Gas Stops.

Don't pass up a chance to buy gas. If you think you may need it soon, buy it now. Don't think "I'll stop in the next town". The next town may be 70 miles away. Buy gas too often. It's better than too seldom, and it beats walking.

Off Road Riding.

Unless you are riding a dual purpose bike and are prepared to camp, stay on established roads. The desert is very treacherous and will bury your bike up to the axles in an instant. I have broken both my ankles riding street bikes on Arizona dirt roads. Learn from my mistakes. It's hard to look macho when you're laying under your bike.

If you know you are going off the beaten path, carry lots of water. Drink it. Don't hoard it. It doesn't do any good in the bottle. If you get lost or stuck in the desert, stay with your bike. Don't try to walk out. Use the mirrors to flash at aircraft. Use gasoline to start a signal fire. Don't burn the bike! You may need it later.

Sun Protection.

The Arizona summertime sun can be intense. Drink lots of water and be sure to wear sun block on your arms, face, and all other exposed skin. If you normally use sun block 10 or 15, move up to 25 or 35. Wear lightweight gloves to protect the backs of your hands. It also helps to wear a lightweight jacket as it will trap your body moisture and help keep you cool.

Helmets.

I suggest you wear a helmet, even if you plan to ride in a state where they're not required. If you will be riding a bike with a windshield, you won't have to wear a face shield on the helmet. On the other hand, you should have a visor on your helmet to shade your eyes. The Arizona sun can be very bright, especially in the mornings and evenings when it is low on the horizon.

Breakdowns and Emergency Equipment.

If it was easy, <u>everyone</u> would be doing it!

It wasn't very long ago when we accepted (Ha! Expected!) on any ride the bike might break down. Those were the "Good Old Days" when we carried spare rectifiers, points, diodes, chain master links, wire, tape, tire tubes, and assorted nuts and bolts in addition to our tool kits. We used to say, "If you can't fix it, you shouldn't ride it."

It's a lot better now. Bikes still break down, but it's the exception rather than the rule. Bikes are so dependable now that the owners don't have to know anything about the inner workings of the machine, much less how to fix them. Also, thanks to new electrical technology, tubeless tires, shafts, and belts, most of the individual parts I listed above, rectifiers, points, diodes, master links, and tire tubes are things of the past. And I say, "Good riddance."

However, as I said, bikes still break down, so I equip all my bikes with the following emergency items:

Tool kit.
Flashlight
Flat tire repair kit.
Spare fuses.
Air pressure gauge.
Taillight bulb.
Headlight bulb.
Chain and lock.
Bike cover.
A full set of spare keys.
A bottle of water (for the riders, not the bike).
A small first aid kit.
A $20.00 bill, two quarters, a dime and a nickel. (In case I lose my wallet)

So, take a few minutes now and think about what your options are if you are merrily rolling down the road and your bike goes silent. Remember, you may well find yourself 100 miles from the nearest anyplace when it happens, and that's no time to start planning.

First, try to fix the bike. Check for blown fuses, clogged gas lines, fouled plugs. Do everything you can to get it running again. But if it just won't go, it's time to go to Plan B.

- Try to flag down a police officer, a truck driver, or a car driver, in that order. Ask them if they would please go to the nearest town and send back a **flatbed** tow truck. Make sure they understand you need a flatbed tow truck. The old fashioned "chain and lift" trucks can cause a lot of damage to your bike and should only be used if a flatbed truck is not available.

- If you flag down a trucker, ask him or her to please pass a message back to you, via other truckers, on their CB radios, to let you know help is on the way.

- Be very selective when accepting "a ride to the next town." I love humanity, but I don't generally trust strangers. Yes, most of them are wonderful (and I've met some really nice ones) but there are also some very weird people out there.

- Stay with your passenger. If you decide to accept a ride, both of you go. There is safety in numbers, not much, but more that if he or she is alone. Don't send your passenger off alone, and don't leave him or her with the bike "to protect it." Your possessions can be replaced. Your passenger cannot.

- If you are going to leave the bike, try to hide it off the road to protect it and your belongings from theft.

- Write down the highway mile marker number so you can find it later, or so you can send the tow truck directly to the bike.

- If you are leaving the bike, and have a bike cover with you, cover the bike. It will make it less attractive to passing motorists.

- Leave the bike on the side stand, not the center stand. It will be more stable and less likely to be blown over by a passing eighteen wheeler.

- If you can't find a towing service to pick up the bike, rent a truck and go get it yourself.

- Once you've transported the bike to the nearest town, use the Telephone Directory (Yellow Pages) to locate a bike shop to do the repairs.

Now, **this is the most important part.** Adjust your mental attitude to, "what the heck, it's an adventure." Don't let the breakdown ruin your vacation. There's no value gained by being upset. Look for something to do. Ask the local folks about the best restaurants, or go see a movie. Relax, kick back, smell some roses. If you are going to be stuck for a few days, rent a car! See some of the sights you were going to see on the bike. It won't be as much fun, but it beats sitting in a motel room.

I remember one breakdown in the world's smallest town in Colorado when Cheryl and I found a tiny little restaurant and had the greatest homemade peach pie I've ever tasted. Now, I'd rather the bike hadn't failed, but on the other hand, I still remember that pie!

Ten Foot Wash Job.

I like to ride a clean bike. I'm convinced they ride smoother, run faster, and break down less. So I do a "ten foot wash job" every morning while on tour. It only takes a few minutes.

I fill one of the motel room's trash cans with warm water, dump in one of those free bottles of shampoo they give you, and take it outside and soap down the bike. Then I rinse the bike with another trash can full of water and wipe it off with a full size towel. The result is a bike that looks good if you don't get any closer than ten feet.

I use a washcloth and towel I bring along just for this purpose. I never use the motel's towels as I'd like to be welcomed back someday. Also, the motels I stay at are mostly small businesses and I worry they might start turning away motorcyclists if I mess up their towels. That would be a real shame.

If you don't have a cloth with you, ask for one at the front desk. They'll be happy to provide you with one, and will probably even offer you the use of their water hose. It's in their best interests after all. They get a happy guest and at the same time safeguard their good towels!

Suggested One Week Tours.

One Week Tour 1. Northern Arizona and a Bit of Colorado.

This is a great tour! See the best parts of Northern Arizona, and the very best part of Southwestern Colorado. Visit Sedona and Oak Creek Canyon on your way to the Grand Canyon. Then pop over to Colorado and ride the Million Dollar Highway and see Mesa Verde.

On your way back into Arizona stop at the Four Corners Monument. It's the only place in America where four states come together. If you stoop down in the middle of the monument you can have your hands and feet in four different states all at the same time!

Turning south, take the Indian guided truck tour through Canyon de Chelly (pronounced "Canyon d' Shay") and see some of the oldest Hohokam Indian ruins in Arizona. White House ruin is magnificent! Then ride along the rim of the canyon and see Spider Rock, the towering spire featured in the movie Poltergeist II.

Leaving Chinle, visit the Hubbell Trading Post. This is a real trading post! Not a tourist attraction. It is the oldest continually operating Indian Trading Post in America.

Ride south and ride through the Petrified Forest. This is 26 miles of great views! Finally, ride the magnificent Mogollon Rim (Mogy-yon Rim) or the Salt River Canyon as you ride from Show Low to Phoenix.

See the "Town to Town Day Rides" section for the details of each of the following day rides.

1. Phoenix	Sedona	169
2. Sedona	Grand Canyon	94
3. Grand Canyon	Cortez	291
4. Cortez	Durango	193
5. Durango	Chinle	228
6. Chinle	Show Low	175
7. Show Low	Phoenix	168

		1318 Miles.

One Week Tour 2. Northern and Southern Arizona.

Have you already visited the Grand Canyon, but not Canyon de Chelly? This is a great tour for you. Ride north through Prescott, Sedona, and Oak Creek Canyon, and then cut across to the northeast to Chinle and Canyon de Chelly.

Take the Indian guided truck tour through Canyon de Chelly (pronounced "Canyon d' Shay") and walk in some of the oldest Hohokam Indian ruins in Arizona. White House ruin is magnificent! Then ride along the rim of the canyon and see Spider Rock, the towering spire featured in the movie Poltergeist II. Leaving Chinle, visit the Hubbell Trading Post. This is real! Not a tourist attraction. The Hubbell Trading Post is the oldest continually operating Indian Trading Post in America.

Head south and ride through the Petrified Forest. This is 26 miles of great views! Heading farther south will bring you to the Chiricahua Mountains, the hiding hills used by the great Indian leaders Geronimo and Cochise. While in the Southeast, visit Tombstone, the town too tough to die! Walk in the actual OK Corral. It's real, not a movie set. This is where the Clantons and the Earps really shot it out!

Ride west a bit and spend a day in Tucson, the "Old Pueblo." This is the oldest continually inhabited city in America. See Mission del Bac, the oldest Spanish Mission in America. On your return to Phoenix, stop off in Florence and visit the prison museum. It has a bizarre collection of used hangman's ropes!

See the "Town to Town Day Rides" section for the details of each of the following day rides.

1. Phoenix	Sedona	169
2. Sedona	Chinle	210
3. Chinle	Show Low	175
4. Show Low	Willcox	191
5. Willcox	Tucson	224
6. Tucson	Tucson	50
7. Tucson	Phoenix	128

		1147

One Week Tour 3. Northwest Arizona and Las Vegas, NV.

Want to visit the ultimate Glitter City? See Las Vegas, the town that never sleeps. On your way, enjoy the Grand Canyon and Hoover Dam, two of the most magnificent attractions in the world. On your way back into Arizona stop off at Lake Havasu and visit London Bridge. Yes, the real London Bridge. It was bought, dismantled, shipped to Arizona, and put back together!

Ride south and visit the pyramid grave site of Hi Jolly, an Egyptian camel driver. His story is fascinating, and well told on a large sign by the grave site. Ride a bit farther south and see the historic Yuma Territorial Prison. You'll be amazed at its starkness, and wonder how anyone ever survived it.

Head east from Yuma and spend a day in Tucson. See the Pima Air Museum, the Old Tucson Movie Town, the Desert Sonoran Museum, or the Titan Missile Silo. Then ride north through Florence (see the museum!) and return to Phoenix.

See the "Town to Town Day Rides" section for the details of each of the following day rides.

1. Phoenix	Williams	184
2. Williams	Williams	122
3. Williams	Las Vegas	227
4. Las Vegas	Lake Havasu	198
5. Lake Havasu	Yuma	153
6. Yuma	Tucson	294
7. Tucson	Phoenix	128

		1153

One Week Tour 4. Eastern and Southeastern Arizona.

This tour includes some of the most magnificent riding roads in Arizona. Ride the Mogollon Rim to Show Low, then up through the Petrified Forest and back to Eagar. Head south on Route 191 to Willcox and see the Chiricahua Mountains and the Old Western towns of Tombstone and Bisbee.

After all that riding, relax for a day or so and see some of the local sights around the "Old Pueblo", Tucson. See the Pima Air Museum, the Sonoran Desert Museum, Old Tucson Movie Town, Saguaro National Monument, Mission del Bac, the Titan Missile Silo, or Kitt Peak. There are enough interesting things to do around Tucson to spend a full week and not get half done.

See the "Town to Town Day Rides" section for the details of each of the following day rides.

1. Phoenix	Show Low	168
2. Show Low	Eagar	193
3. Eagar	Willcox	202
4. Willcox	Bisbee	200
5. Bisbee	Tucson	112
6. Tucson	Tucson	50
7. Tucson	Phoenix	128

		1053

Suggested Two Week Tours.

Two Week Tour 1. Arizona and a Bit of Colorado.

This is a tour to remember for the rest of your life! Two weeks of the best of the best. The best of Arizona and the best of Colorado. Spend a few days in Northern Arizona and then shoot over to Colorado for a couple of days of magnificent mountain riding on the Million Dollar Highway. Return to Arizona and ride from the northeast to the Southeast on some of the best riding roads you'll ever see. Head due West for some wide open, horizon to horizon riding. This is BIG country!

Here are just some of the interesting places on this tour.

Wickenburg, Prescott, Jerome (Ghost Town), Sedona, The Grand Canyon, Monument Valley, The Million Dollar Highway, Mesa Verde, Four Corners, Canyon de Chelly, the Petrified Forest, Route 191, Dos Cabezas (Ghost Town), the Chiricahua Mountains, Bisbee, Tombstone, Tucson, the Mission del Bac, the Pima Air Museum, the Sonoran Desert Museum, Old Tucson Movie Town, the Historic Yuma Territorial Prison, London Bridge, Oatman (Ghost Town), Historic Route 66, and the Tonto Natural Bridge.

See the "Town to Town Day Rides" section for the details of each of the following day rides.

1. Phoenix	Sedona	169
2. Sedona	Grand Canyon	94
3. Grand Canyon	Cortez	291
4. Cortez	Durango	193
5. Durango	Chinle	228
6. Chinle	Show Low	175
7. Show Low	Willcox	191
8. Willcox	Tucson	224
9. Tucson	Tucson	100
10. Tucson	Tucson	100
11. Tucson	Yuma	294
12. Yuma	Lake Havasu	153
13. Lake Havasu	Williams	210
14. Williams	Phoenix	184

		2606

Two Week Tour 2. North, East, South, and West Arizona.

Ride some of the best parts of Northern Arizona including both the South and North Rims of the Grand Canyon on this tour. Then take a short side trip into Utah as you ride through Monument Valley. Return to Arizona, visit our other famous canyon, Canyon de Chelly, and then ride from northeast Arizona to the southeast on some of America's best motorcycling roads. Relax for a few days in Tucson and then head due West for some open country riding to Yuma and Lake Havasu.

Here are just some of the interesting places on this tour.

Wickenburg, Prescott, Jerome (Ghost Town), Sedona, The Grand Canyon South Rim, the Grand Canyon North Rim, Monument Valley, Canyon de Chelly, the Petrified Forest, Route 191, Dos Cabezas (Ghost Town), the Chiricahua Mountains, Bisbee, Tombstone, Tucson, the Mission del Bac, the Pima Air Museum, the Sonoran Desert Museum, Old Tucson Movie Town, the Historic Yuma Territorial Prison, London Bridge, Oatman (Ghost Town), Historic Route 66, and Williams.

See the "Town to Town Day Rides" section for the details of each of the following day rides.

1.	Phoenix	Sedona	169
2.	Sedona	Grand Canyon	94
3.	Grand Canyon	Grand Canyon	213
4.	Grand Canyon	Mexican Hat	244
5.	Mexican Hat	Chinle	124
6.	Chinle	Show Low	175
7.	Show Low	Willcox	191
8.	Willcox	Tucson	224
9.	Tucson	Tucson	100
10.	Tucson	Tucson	100
11.	Tucson	Yuma	294
12.	Yuma	Lake Havasu	153
13.	Lake Havasu	Williams	210
14.	Williams	Phoenix	184

2475

Maps.

The following maps are intended to be used in conjunction with a standard, full size, full detail Arizona state road map. The day rides refer to these maps.

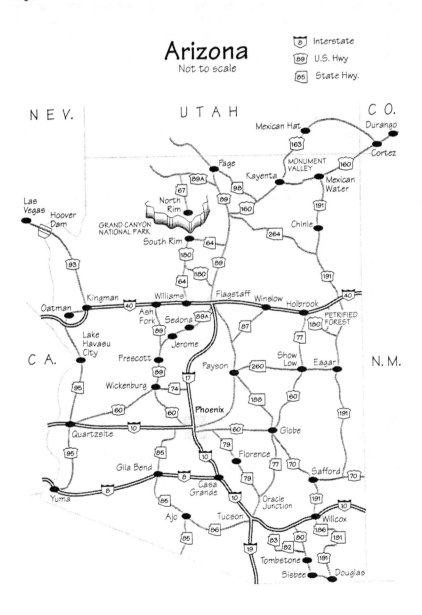

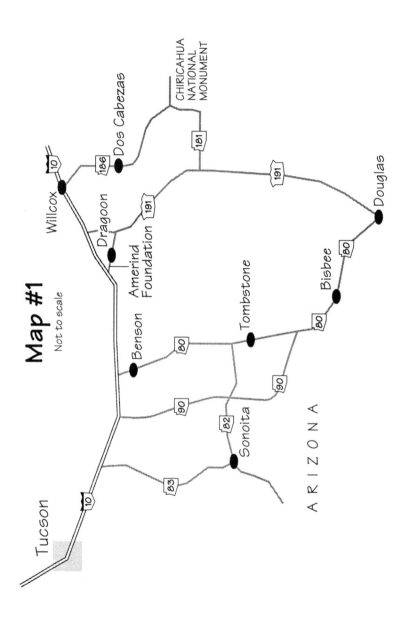

Map #1
Not to scale

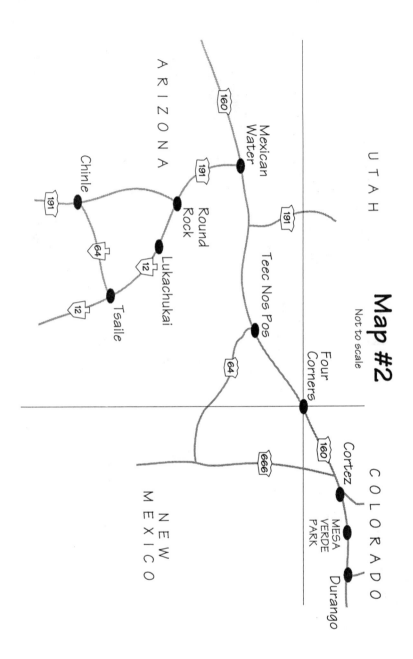

Map #3

Not to scale

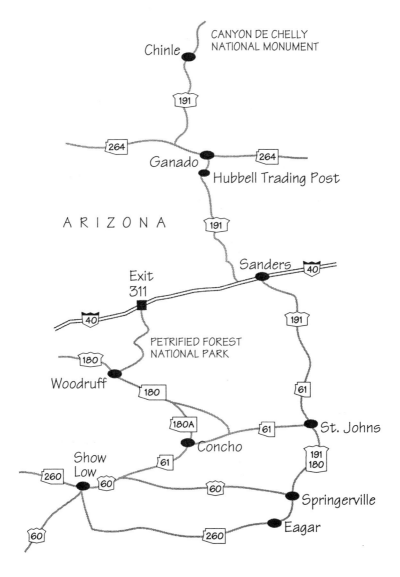

CANYON DE CHELLY
NATIONAL MONUMENT

Chinle

191

264

Ganado

264

Hubbell Trading Post

A R I Z O N A

191

Sanders

40

Exit
311

40

191

PETRIFIED FOREST
NATIONAL PARK

180

Woodruff

180

180A

61

St. Johns

Concho

61

191
180

Show
Low

260

61

60

60

Springerville

60

260

Eagar

Map #4

Not to scale

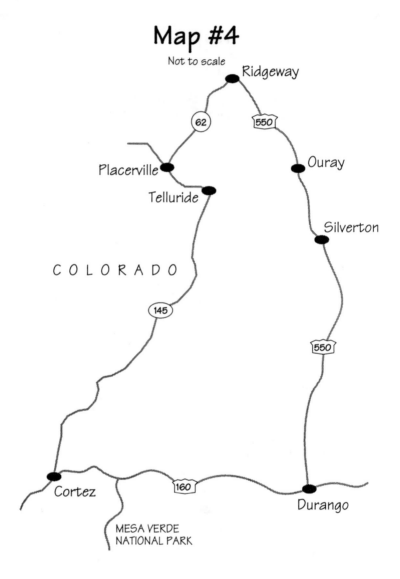

Ridgeway

62

550

Placerville

Ouray

Telluride

Silverton

C O L O R A D O

145

550

Cortez

160

Durango

MESA VERDE
NATIONAL PARK

Map #5

Not to scale

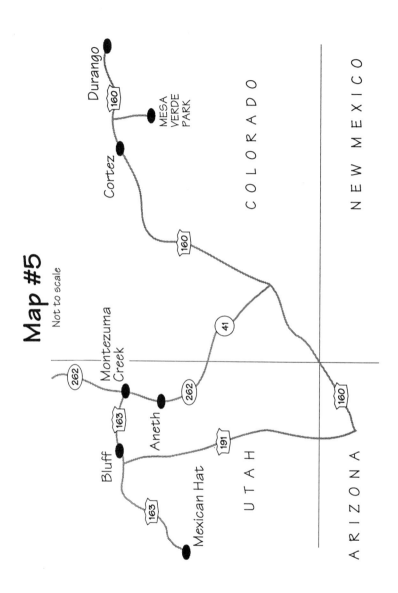

Map #6

Not to scale

Map #7

Not to scale

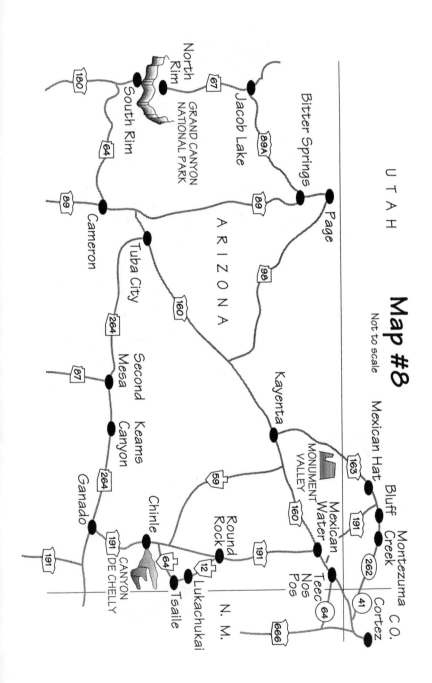

Map #8

Not to scale

Map #9

Not to scale

Map #10

Not to scale

Map #11

Not to scale

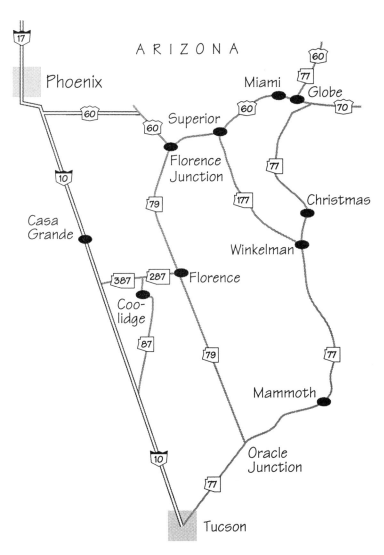

Map #12

Not to scale

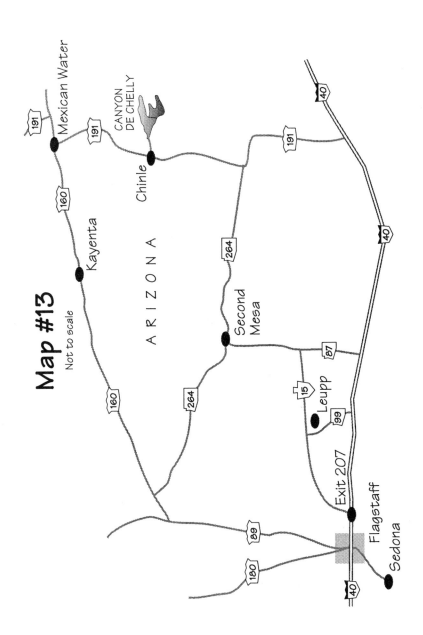

Map #13
Not to scale

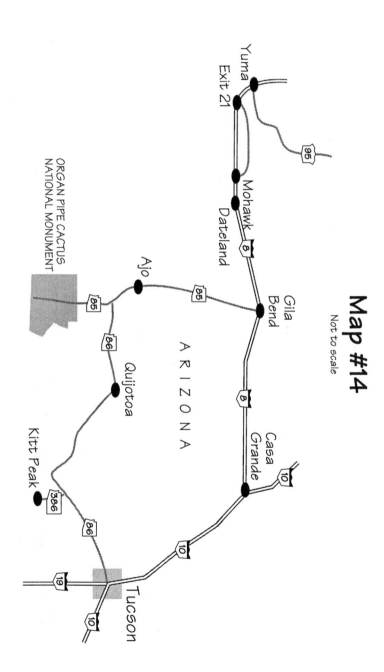

Map #14

Not to scale

Yuma
Exit 21

95

Mohawk
Dateland
8

ORGAN PIPE CACTUS
NATIONAL MONUMENT

Ajo
85
85
86

Gila
Bend

ARIZONA

Quijotoa

8

Casa
Grande

10

Kitt Peak
386
86

10

19
10

Tucson

Town to Town Day Rides.

For Motorcyclists...
   the ride is the objective.
      The destination is the excuse.

The following day rides use the most scenic routes between destination towns. There are often more direct routes but they're not as much fun. The miles listed are reasonably accurate, depending on your starting and ending points in the actual towns, but the hours are very subjective.

I've tried to estimate how long it should take you to ride each trip if you take time to smell the flowers and see some of the local area attractions. If you race you can ride them faster, and if you really enjoy some of the points of interest it will take you longer. Figure 3 to 4 hours a day for sightseeing., with the rest of the time being riding hours. All these tours are on paved rural highways. There are only a few sections of unpaved road.

- Off the paved highway in Monument Valley. (Don't do it.)

- Off the paved road anywhere else. (Don't do it.)

- The last few hundred feet into the parking lot at the Vulture Mine in Wickenburg.

- The three mile access road from the highway to the Tonto Natural Bridge, south of Strawberry, AZ. This steep, downhill road is graded from time to time and they add fresh gravel. Stop at the top and check it out on foot. If it seems to be deep in loose gravel or stones, skip it. Once you've committed to going down, there is no way to turn around. Be extra careful at the bottom as you approach the Ranger Station, it's not as level as it looks. The good news is that paving is scheduled for late 1994.

Other than that you should have no trouble riding these tours. So relax and enjoy yourself.

Day Ride : **Bisbee to Tucson. (112 mi)**
Hours   : 6
Map   : See Map #1.
Highlights : Tombstone.
             Tucson.

Leave Bisbee on Rt. 80 North.	
Ride 24 miles to Tombstone.	
Ride 3 miles to Rt. 82.	Turn left (West).
Ride 36 miles to Sonoita.	Turn right onto Rt. 83 North.
Ride 27 miles to I-10.	Turn left onto I-10 West.
Ride 22 miles to Tucson.	

Map #1
Not to scale

Day Ride : **Bisbee to Willcox via Douglas. (200 mi)**
Hours : 4-5
Map : See Map #1.
Highlights : Chiricahua National Monument.
               The Amerind Foundation.
               Dos Cabezas. (Ghost Town)

Leave Bisbee on Rt. 80 South/East.	
Ride 25 miles to Douglas.	Turn left onto Rt. 191 North.
Ride 38 miles to Rt. 191/181 Intersection.	Stay left on Rt. 191.
Ride 18 miles to the road to Dragoon. (No Rt. Number)	Turn left (West).
Ride 10 miles to Dragoon.	
Ride 2 miles to Amerind Foundation. This foundation displays the finest collection of Indian artifacts in Arizona.	
When you leave the Amerind Foundation, ride East towards Dragoon.	
Ride 2 miles to Dragoon.	
Ride 10 miles to Rt. 191.	Turn right (South).
Ride 18 miles to Rt. 181.	Turn left (East).
Ride 23 miles to Chiricahua National Monument.	Turn right.
Ride 11 miles into Chiricahua National Monument.	
Ride 11 miles out of Chiricahua National Monument.	
When you leave the Chiricahua National Monument,	Turn right onto Rt. 186.
Ride 17 miles to Dos Cabezas.	
Ride 15 miles to Willcox.	

Day Ride : **Chinle to Cortez, CO. (145 mi)**
Hours   : 6
Map   : See Map #8.
Highlights : Four Corners Monument.

Leave Chinle on Indian Rt. 64 North/East. This will give you some great views down into Canyon de Chelly.	
Ride 24 miles through Tsaile.	Bear left at the fork in the road.
Ride 22 miles (through Lukachukai) to Round Rock. Intersect with Rt. 191.	Turn right (North) onto Rt. 191.
Ride 30 miles to Mexican Water.	Turn right (East) onto Rt. 160.
Ride 30 miles to Four Corners Monument. This is the only place in America where you can stand in four states at once.	
Ride 5 miles to intersection of Rt. 41/160. Stay on Rt. 160.	
Ride 14 miles to Rt. 191 (666).	Turn left (North).
Ride 20 miles to Cortez.	

Day Ride : **Chinle to Show Low. (175 mi)**
Hours : 8-10
Map : See Map #3.
Highlights : Hubbell Trading Post
Petrified Forest

Leave Chinle on Rt. 191 South.	
Ride 31 miles to intersect with Rt. 264.	Turn left (East).
Ride 7 miles to Ganado.	Turn right (South) on Rt. 191.
Ride 2 miles to Hubbell Trading Post. Plan on spending 1-2 hours at the Hubbell Trading Post. Take the tour of Mr. Hubbell's house.	
Ride 31 miles to Interstate 40.	Turn right (West).
Ride 23 miles to the Petrified Forest. (Exit 311)	
Ride 26 miles through the Petrified Forest to Rt. 180. Plan on spending 2-3 hours in the Petrified Forest.	When you leave the Petrified Forest, turn left onto Rt. 180.
Ride 15 miles to where the road splits.	Bear right onto Rt. 180A.
Ride 10 miles to Concho. The road merges with Rt. 61.	Bear to the right onto Rt. 61.
Ride 19 miles to intersect with Rt. 60.	Bear right (West).
Ride 11 miles to Show Low.	

Day Ride : **Cortez, CO to Chinle. (145 mi)**
Hours   : 7
Map   : See Map #2.
Highlights : Four Corners.
             Canyon de Chelly.
Cautions   : Call ahead. Accommodations are limited.
             Call ahead for Truck Tour of Canyon de Chelly.

Leave Cortez on Rt. 160/191 (666) South/West.	
Ride 20 miles to Rt. 160.	Bear right (West).
Ride 19 miles to the Four Corners monument. This is the only place in America where you can stand in four states at once.	
Ride 6 miles to Teec Nos Pos.	Turn right and stay on Rt. 160 (West).
Ride 24 miles to Mexican Water.	Turn left (South) onto Rt. 191.
Ride 30 miles to Round Rock.	Leave Rt. 191 and bear left onto Indian Rt. 12 (East/South)
Ride 16 miles to Lukachukai.	Bear right. Stay on Indian Rt. 12.
Ride 6 miles to Tsaile.	Turn right onto Indian Rt. 64.
Ride 24 miles to Chinle.	

Day Ride : **Cortez, CO to Durango, CO. Million Dollar Highway.**
(193 mi)
Hours : 8 to 10
Map : See Map #4.
Highlights : The Million Dollar Highway.

Leave Cortez on Rt. 145 (North)	
Ride 76 miles to Telluride.	
Ride 13 miles to Placerville.	Turn right (North) onto Rt. 62.
Ride 25 miles to Ridgeway.	Turn right (South) onto Rt. 550.
Ride 11 miles to Ouray. (Pronounced "You-Ray")	
Ride 23 miles to Silverton.	
Ride 45 miles to Durango.	

Map #4

Not to scale

Day Ride : **Durango, CO to Chinle. (228 mi)**
Hours   : 10
Map   : See Map #2.
Highlights : Mesa Verde National Park.
             Four Corners.
             Canyon de Chelly.
Cautions   : Call ahead. Accommodations are limited.
             Call ahead for Truck Tour of Canyon de Chelly.

Leave Durango on Rt. 160 West.	
Ride 34 miles to Mesa Verde National Park.	
Ride 38 miles up and back in Mesa Verde. This is a beautiful ride.	
Ride 11 miles to Cortez.	Bear left (South) onto Rt. 160/666.
Ride 20 miles to where Rt. 160 turns right.	Turn right (West) and stay on Rt. 160.
Ride 19 miles to the Four Corners monument. This is the only place in America where you can stand in four states at once.	
Ride 6 miles to Teec Nos Pos.	Turn right and stay on Rt. 160 (West).
Ride 24 miles to Mexican Water.	Turn left (South) onto Rt. 191.
Ride 30 miles to Round Rock.	Turn left onto Indian Rt. 12 (East/South)
Ride 16 miles to Lukachukai.	Bear to the right and stay on Indian Rt. 12.
Ride 6 miles to Tsaile.	Turn right onto Indian Rt. 64.
Ride 24 miles to Chinle.	

Day Ride : **Durango, CO to Mexican Hat, UT. (190 mi)**
Hours : 10
Map : See Map #5 and Map #8.
Highlights : Mesa Verde National Park

Leave Durango on Rt. 160 West.	
Ride 34 miles to Mesa Verde National Park.	
Ride 38 miles up and back in Mesa Verde. This is a beautiful ride.	
Ride 11 miles to Cortez.	Bear left (South) onto Rt. 160/666.
Ride 20 miles to where Rt. 160 turns right.	Turn right (West) and stay on Rt. 160.
Ride 20 miles to Rt. 41.	Turn right onto Rt.41 (North).
Ride 10 miles to the Utah border. Rt. 41 changes to Rt. 262 at the border.	
Ride 22 miles to Montezuma Creek.	Turn left (South onto Rt. 163)
Ride 12 miles to Bluff	
Ride 23 miles to Mexican Hat.	

Map #5

Not to scale

UTAH
COLORADO
ARIZONA
NEW MEXICO

Day Ride   : Eagar to Chinle via the Petrified Forest. (239 mi)
Hours   : 7
Map   : See Map #3.
Highlights   : The Petrified Forest.
                Canyon de Chelly
Cautions   : Call ahead. Accommodations are limited.
                Call ahead for Truck Tour of Canyon de Chelly.

Leave Eagar on Rt. 260 West.	
Ride 58 miles to Show Low.	Turn right onto Rt. 60 North/East.
Ride 11 miles to Rt. 61.	Turn left onto Rt. 61 North.
Ride 19 miles to Concho.	Turn left onto Rt. 180A (North).
Ride 25 miles to Woodruff.	Turn right and enter the Petrified Forest.
Ride 26 miles through Petrified Forest.	Turn right onto I-40 East.
Ride 23 miles to Rt. 191.	Turn left onto Rt. 191 North.
Ride 39 miles to Ganado. Consider visiting the Hubbell Trading Post as you go by. It's worth seeing. Plan on spending 1-2 hours at the Hubbell Trading Post. Take the tour of Mr. Hubbell's house.	Turn left onto Rt. 191/264 West.
Ride 7 miles to Rt. 191.	Turn right onto Rt. 191.
Ride 31 miles to Chinle.	

Day Ride : **Eagar to Chinle via Rt. 191. (159 mi)**
Hours : 6
Map : See Map #3.
Highlights : Rt. 191. A beautiful motorcycling road.
Canyon de Chelly.
Cautions : Call ahead. Accommodations are limited.
Call ahead for Truck Tour of Canyon de Chelly.

Leave Eagar on Rt. 180/191 North.	
Ride 25 miles to St. Johns.	Merge onto Rt. 61/191 North.
Ride 52 miles to Sanders.	Turn left onto I-40 West.
Ride 5 miles to Rt. 191.	Turn right onto Rt. 191 North.
Ride 39 miles to Ganado. Consider visiting the Hubbell Trading Post as you go by. It's worth seeing. Plan on spending 1-2 hours at the Hubbell Trading Post. Take the tour of Mr. Hubbell's house.	Turn left onto Rt. 264 West.
Ride 7 miles to Rt. 191.	Turn right onto Rt. 191.
Ride 31 miles to Chinle.	

Day Ride : **Eagar to Willcox. (202 mi)**
Hours   : 8-10
Map   : See Map #6.
Highlights : The ride down Rt. 191!

Leave Eagar on Rt. 180/191 South.	
Ride 27 miles to Alpine.	Bear to the right and stay on Rt. 191.
Ride 83 miles to Morenci.	
Ride 7 miles to Clifton.	
Ride 9 miles to Threeway.	Turn right (West) onto Rt. 191.
Ride 24 miles to connect with Rt. 70.	Turn right onto Rt. 70.
Ride 7 miles to Safford.	Turn left onto Rt. 191.
Ride 33 miles to I-10.	Turn right onto I-10 West.
Ride 12 miles to Willcox.	

Grave site (foreground) on the Coronado Trail

(see story page 121 - Photo by author)

Day Ride : **Flagstaff to Phoenix via Sedona. (190 mi)**
Hours : 8-10
Map : See Map #7.
Highlights : Wickenburg
           Yarnell Hill and the Shrine of St. Joseph.
           Prescott - The Capitol Building.
           Prescott - Sharlot Hall Museum.
           Jerome (Ghost Town)
           Tuzigoot Indian Ruins
           Sedona

Leave Flagstaff on Rt. 89A South toward Sedona.	
Ride 25 miles to Sedona.	At Rt. 89A and Rt. 179, turn right and stay on Rt. 89A.
Ride 13 miles to Cottonwood.	At Rt. 89A and Rt. 260, turn right and stay on Rt. 89A.
Ride 3 miles to the Tuzigoot Ruins. These are some of the best Indian ruins in Arizona. Well worth seeing.	
Stay on Rt. 89A and ride 6 miles to Jerome. Plan on spending a couple of hours in Jerome.	
Leave Jerome on Rt. 89A and ride 26 miles to Rt. 89.	Turn left (West) onto Rt. 89.
Ride 7 miles to Prescott.	Stay on Rt. 89 through town.
Ride 31 miles to Yarnell.	Be careful on Yarnell Hill!
Ride 9 miles to Congress and Rt. 71. Watch for "Frog Rock" just north of Congress.	Bear left and stay on Rt. 89.
Ride 10 miles to Rt. 93.	Turn left onto Rt. 93.
Ride 6 miles to Wickenburg.	Turn left onto Rt. 93.
Ride 11 miles to Rt. 74.	Turn left (West).
Ride 31 miles to I-17.	Turn right (South).
Ride 20 miles to Phoenix.	

Day Ride : **Flagstaff to Phoenix via Payson. (162 mi)**
Hours : 6
Map : See Map #7.
Highlights : Strawberry Schoolhouse.
             The bar/restaurant behind Mormon Lake.
             Tonto Natural Bridge.

Leave Flagstaff on I-17 South toward Phoenix. After leaving Flagstaff follow the signs to the Flagstaff Airport to get onto Lake Mary Road (Forest Highway 3) (South/East).

Ride 15 miles to Mormon Lake.	Ride the 2 mile loop behind the lake. There's a neat cowboy bar and restaurant with good food.

Ride about 15 miles to and through Happy Jack.

Ride 11 miles to Clint's Well.	Turn right (South) onto Rt. 87

Ride 5 miles to Rt. 260, the Camp Verde turn off.
This is also known as the General Crook Highway.

*** Alternate ***

If you are in a hurry to get back to Phoenix, turn right (West) onto Rt. 260 and ride to Camp Verde. This is a very nice motorcycling road. Then turn left onto Interstate 17 and blast south to Phoenix.

Stay on Rt. 87, ride past the Camp Verde turn off and continue on 16 miles to Strawberry.

Ride 2 miles to Pine.

Ride 5 miles to the Tonto Natural Bridge.	This is worth seeing, but be very careful on the road down. Read about it in the Arizona Attractions section of this book.

Ride 10 miles to Payson.

Stay on Rt. 87 and ride 85 miles to Phoenix.

Day Ride : **Grand Canyon North Rim to Mexican Hat, UT. (244 mi)**
Hours : 8
Map : See Map #8.
Highlights : Monument Valley.

Leave the North Rim on Rt. 67 North.	
Ride 44 miles to Jacob Lake.	Turn right (East) onto Rt. 89A.
Ride 51 miles to Bitter Springs.	Turn left onto Rt. 89 to Page.
Ride 17 miles to Page.	Turn right onto Rt. 98 East.
Ride 59 miles to Rt. 160.	Turn left onto Rt. 160 East.
Ride 32 miles to Kayenta.	Turn left onto Rt. 163.
Ride 41 miles to Mexican Hat, Utah.	

Day Ride : **Grand Canyon North Rim to South Rim. (213 mi)**
Hours : 8
Map : See Map #8.
Highlights : The Grand Canyon
26 Mile Scenic Ride.

Leave the North Rim on Rt. 67 North.	
Ride 44 miles to Jacob Lake.	Turn right (East) onto Rt. 89A.
Ride 51 miles to Bitter Springs.	Merge right (South) onto Rt. 89.
Ride 61 miles to Cameron.	Turn right (West) onto Rt. 64.
Ride 57 miles to Grand Canyon South Rim.	

Day Ride : **Grand Canyon South Rim to North Rim. (213 mi)**
Hours   : 8
Map   : See Map #8.
Highlights : Grand Canyon.
                  26 mile Scenic Ride.

Leave the Grand Canyon on Rt. 64, the 26 mile scenic drive.	
Ride 26 miles on the scenic drive. The first two overlooks are the best for "me and my bike at the Grand Canyon photos."	
Ride 31 miles to Cameron.	Turn left onto Rt. 89 North.
Ride 14 miles to Rt. 89/160 Intersection.	Stay left on Rt. 89.
Ride 47 miles to Bitter Springs.	Stay left on Rt. 89A.
Ride 51 miles to Jacob Lake.	Turn left onto Rt. 67 South.
Ride 44 miles to the North Rim.	

Grand Canyon — South Rim View
(Photo courtesy Arizona Office of Tourism)

Day Ride : **Grand Canyon South Rim to Chinle. (236 mi)**
Hours : 8
Map : See Map #8.
Highlights : Canyon de Chelly.
Cautions : Call ahead. Accommodations are limited.
        Call ahead for Truck Tour of Canyon de Chelly.

Leave the Grand Canyon on Rt. 64, the 26 mile scenic drive.	
Ride 26 miles on the scenic drive. The first two overlooks are the best for "me and my bike at the Grand Canyon photos."	
Ride 31 miles to Cameron.	Turn left onto Rt. 89 North.
Ride 14 miles to Rt. 160.	Turn right (East).
Ride 10 miles to Tuba City.	Turn right onto Rt. 264 South.
Ride 66 miles to Second Mesa.	
Ride 18 miles to Keams Canyon.	
Ride 40 miles to Ganado.	Turn left onto Rt. 191 North.
Ride 31 miles to Chinle.	

Day Ride : **Grand Canyon South Rim to Cortez, CO. (291 mi)**
Hours   : 8-10 via Monument Valley.
Map   : See Map #8.
Highlights : Monument Valley

Leave the Grand Canyon on Rt. 64, the 26 mile scenic drive.	
Ride 26 miles on the scenic drive. The first two overlooks are the best for "me and my bike at the Grand Canyon photos."	
Ride 31 miles to Cameron.	Turn left onto Rt. 89 North.
Ride 14 miles to Rt. 160.	Turn right (East).
Ride 10 miles to Tuba City.	
Ride 72 miles to Kayenta.	Turn left onto Rt. 163.
Ride 41 miles through Monument Valley to Mexican Hat, Utah.	
Ride 23 miles to Bluff.	
Ride 12 miles to Montezuma Creek.	Turn right onto Rt. 262.
Ride 22 miles to Utah/Colorado border. Rt. 262 becomes Rt. 41 when you cross into Colorado.	
Ride 10 miles to Rt. 160.	Turn left (East) onto Rt. 160.
Ride 20 miles to Rt. 160/666.	Bear left (North).
Ride 20 miles to Cortez.	

Day Ride : **Grand Canyon South Rim to Cortez, CO. (263 mi)**
Hours : 8 via Four Corners.
Map : See Map #8.
Highlights : Four Corners

Leave the Grand Canyon on Rt. 64, the 26 mile scenic drive.	
Ride 26 miles on the scenic drive. The first two overlooks are the best for "me and my bike at the Grand Canyon photos."	
Ride 31 miles to Cameron.	Turn left onto Rt. 89 North.
Ride 14 miles to Rt. 160.	Turn right (East) onto Rt. 160.
Ride 10 miles to Tuba City.	
Ride 72 miles to Kayenta.	
Leave Kayenta on Rt. 160 (East).	
Ride 39 miles to Mexican Water.	
Ride 26 miles to Teec Nos Pos.	Turn left and stay on Rt. 160.
Ride 6 miles to Four Corners Monument. This is the only place in America where you can stand in four states at once.	
Ride 5 miles to intersection of Rt. 41/160. Stay on Rt. 160.	
Ride 14 miles to Rt. 160/666.	Turn left (North).
Ride 20 miles to Cortez.	

Day Ride : **Grand Canyon South Rim to Lake Havasu. (273 mi)**
Hours   : 10
Map   : See Map #9.
Highlights : The last segment of Historic Rt. 66.
              The Ghost Town of Oatman.
              London Bridge.

Leave the South Rim on Rt. 180 South.	
Ride 30 miles to Valle, where Rt. 180 and Rt. 64 intersect.	Bear to the right onto Rt. 64 (South).
Ride 29 miles to Williams.	Turn right (West) onto I-40.
Ride 26 miles to Exit 139.	Turn right (West) onto Rt. 66.
Ride 19 miles to Seligman.	
Ride 83 miles to Kingman (Exit 53).	Turn left (South) onto I-40.
Ride 7 miles to Exit 44 (Oatman exit).	This is Rt. 66 again, even if it's not marked 66.
Ride 25 miles to Oatman.	
Ride 23 miles to I-40.	Turn left (East)
Ride 10 miles to Exit 9.	Turn right onto Rt. 95 (South).
Ride 21 miles to Lake Havasu City.	

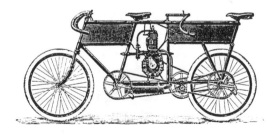

Day Ride : **Grand Canyon South Rim to Las Vegas, NV.** (**303 mi**)
Hours   : 8-10
Map   : See Map #9.
Highlights : The last section of Historic Rt. 66.
               Hoover Dam.
               Las Vegas.

Leave the Grand Canyon on Rt. 180 South.	
Ride 31 miles to Valle.	Turn right (merge) onto Rt. 64 South.
Ride 28 miles to I-40.	Turn right onto I-40 West.
Ride 31 miles to Williams.	Ride through Williams.
Ride 18 miles (Approx) to Exit 139 Ash Fork.	Exit onto Historic Rt. 66.
Ride 19 miles to Seligman.	
Ride 51 miles to Valentine.	
Ride 39 miles to I-40.	Turn right onto I-40 West.
Ride 7 miles to Exit 48.	Turn right onto Rt. 93 North/West.
Ride 53 miles to Hoover Dam. Consider touring the dam. It's really worth the time.	
Ride 7 miles to Boulder City. The film at the visitor's center on the dam construction is worth seeing.	
Ride 19 miles to Las Vegas.	

Day Ride : **Grand Canyon South Rim to Mexican Hat, UT. (194 mi)**
Hours   : 8
Map   : See Map #8.
Highlights : Monument Valley.
           : Gouldings Trading Post.

Leave the Grand Canyon on Rt. 64, the 26 mile scenic drive.	
Ride 26 miles on the scenic drive. The first two overlooks are the best for "me and my bike at the Grand Canyon photos."	
Ride 31 miles to Cameron.	Turn left onto Rt. 89 North.
Ride 14 miles to Rt. 160.	Turn right (East).
Ride 10 miles to Tuba City.	
Ride 72 miles to Kayenta.	Turn left onto Rt. 163.
Ride 23 miles through Monument Valley to Gouldings Trading Post.	
Ride 18 miles through Monument Valley to Mexican Hat, Utah.	

Monument Valley shepherd and his flock
(Photo courtesy Arizona Office of Tourism)

Day Ride : **Lake Havasu to Las Vegas, NV. (160 mi)**
Hours   : 7-10
Map   : See Map #9.
Highlights : Oatman (Ghost Town).
             Hoover Dam.
             Las Vegas.

Leave Lake Havasu on Rt. 95 North.	
Ride 21 miles to I-40.	Turn left onto I-40 West.
Ride 9 miles to Topock.	Turn right onto Rt. 66 to Oatman.
Ride 23 miles to Oatman.	
Ride 25 miles to I-40.	Turn left onto I-40 East.
Ride 3 miles to Kingman.	Turn left onto Rt. 93 North.
Ride 53 miles to Hoover Dam.	
Ride 7 miles to Boulder City.	
Ride 19 miles to Las Vegas.	

Day Ride : **Lake Havasu to Williams. (210 mi)**
Hours   : 8
Map   : See Map #9.
Highlights : Oatman. (Ghost Town)
             The last section of Historic Rt. 66.

Leave Lake Havasu on Rt. 95 North.	
Ride 21 miles to I-40.	Turn left onto I-40 West.
Ride 9 miles to Topock.	Turn right onto Rt. 66 to Oatman.
Ride 23 miles to Oatman.	
Ride 25 miles to I-40.	Turn left onto I-40 East.
Ride 8 miles to Exit 53.	Turn left onto Historic Rt. 66 East.
Ride 32 miles to Valentine.	
Ride 51 miles to Seligman.	
Ride 19 miles to I-40.	Turn left onto I-40 East.
Ride 22 miles to Williams.	

Day Ride   :   **Lake Havasu to Yuma. (153 mi)**
Hours   :   6-7
Map   :   See Map #9.
Highlights :   The Grave of Hi Jolly in Quartzsite.
               The Old Yuma Territorial Prison.

Leave Lake Havasu on Rt. 95 South.
Ride 35 miles to Parker.
Ride 35 miles to Quartzsite.
The Hi Jolly Monument is at the west end of town in the old cemetery. It's poorly marked and the local people don't seem to know about it. Look for a small paved road to the north. It's down the small road about a mile.
Leave Quartzsite on Rt. 95 South.
Ride 83 miles to Yuma.
Visit the Yuma Territorial Prison. It's fascinating.

Map #9
Not to scale

Day Ride : **Las Vegas, NV to Lake Havasu. (198 mi)**
Hours : 6
Map   : See Map #9.
Highlights : Oatman (Ghost Town)
     London Bridge

Leave Las Vegas on Rt. 93/95 South/East toward Boulder City.	
Ride 19 miles toward Boulder City.	Turn right onto Rt. 95 South.
Ride 36 miles to Searchlight.	
Ride 19 miles to Rt. 163/68.	Turn left onto Rt. 163/68 East.
Ride 39 miles to Rt. 93.	Turn right onto Rt. 93.
Ride 3 miles to I-40.	Turn right onto I-40 South/West.
Ride 3 miles to the Oatman exit.	Turn right onto Rt. 66 to Oatman.
Ride 26 miles to Oatman.	
Ride 23 miles to Rt. 95/I-40.	Turn left onto I-40 East.
Ride 9 miles to Rt. 95.	Turn right onto Rt. 95 South.
Ride 21 miles to Lake Havasu.	

London Bridge at Lake Havasu
(Photo courtesy Lake Havasu Chamber of Commerce)

Day Ride : **Las Vegas, NV to Williams. (227 mi)**
Hours : **8**
Map : See Map #9.
Highlights : Hoover Dam.
The Last Section of Historic Rt. 66.

Leave Las Vegas on Rt. 93/95 South/East toward Boulder City.	
Ride 19 miles to Boulder City.	
Ride 7 miles to Hoover Dam.	
Ride 70 miles to Kingman.	Turn left onto I-40 East.
Ride 7 miles to Exit 53.	Turn left onto Historic Rt. 66.
Ride 32 miles to Valentine.	
Ride 51 miles to Seligman.	
Ride 19 miles to Ash Fork.	Turn left onto I-40 (East).
Ride 22 miles to Williams.	

Map #9
Not to scale

Day Ride : **Mexican Hat, UT to Chinle. (124 mi)**
Hours   : 3
Map   : See Map #8.
Highlights : Canyon de Chelly.
Cautions   : Call ahead. Accommodations are limited.
             Call ahead for Truck Tour of Canyon de Chelly.

Leave Mexican Hat on Rt. 163 East.	
Ride 20 miles toward Bluff.	Turn right (South) 3 miles before Bluff, onto Rt. 191.
Ride 23 miles to Rt. 160.	Turn right (West).
Ride 2 miles to Mexican Water.	Turn left (South) onto Rt. 191.
Ride 30 miles to Round Rock.	Turn left onto Indian Rt. 12 (East/South)
Ride 16 miles to Lukachukai.	Bear right and stay on Indian Rt. 12.
Ride 6 miles to Tsaile.	Turn right onto Indian Rt. 64.
Ride 24 miles to Chinle.	

You can look into the canyon from roads along both sides. The only way to go into the canyon is in a six-wheel truck tour run by the local Indians. It's a very interesting tour and well worth doing.

Day Ride : **Mexican Hat, UT to Durango, CO. (190 mi)**
Hours : 10
Map : See Map #5.
Highlights : Mesa Verde National Park

Leave Mexican Hat on Rt. 163 East.	
Ride 23 miles to Bluff.	
Ride 12 miles to Montezuma Creek.	Turn right onto Rt. 262.
Ride 22 miles to the Utah/Colorado border. Rt. 262 turns into Rt. 41.	
Ride 10 miles to Rt. 160.	Turn left (North/East) onto Rt. 160.
Ride 20 miles to where Rt. 160 bears off to the left.	Bear to the left onto Rt. 160.
Ride 20 miles to Cortez.	
Ride 11 miles to Mesa Verde National Park.	
Ride 38 miles up and back in Mesa Verde National Park. It's well worth seeing. When you exit Mesa Verde turn right onto Rt. 160 East.	
Ride 34 miles to Durango.	

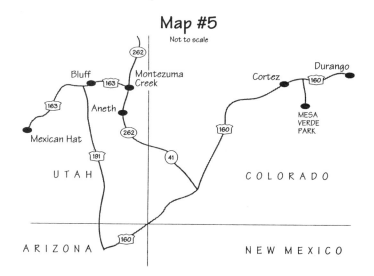

Map #5

Not to scale

Day Ride : **Mexican Hat, UT to Grand Canyon - North Rim. (244 mi)**
Hours   : 10
Map   : See Map #8.
Highlights : Monument Valley.

Leave Mexican Hat on Rt. 163 South.	
Ride 41 miles to Kayenta.	Turn right (West) onto Rt. 160.
Ride 32 miles to Rt. 98.	Turn right (North) onto Rt. 98.
Ride 59 miles to Page.	Turn left onto Rt. 89 South.
Ride 17 miles to Bitter Springs.	Turn right (West) onto Rt. 89A.
Ride 51 miles to Jacob Lake.	Turn left (South) onto Rt. 67.
Ride 44 miles to the North Rim of the Grand Canyon.	

Monument Valley of Northeastern Arizona
(Photo courtesy Arizona Office of Tourism)

Day Ride : **Phoenix to Flagstaff via Sedona. (190 mi)**
Hours : 8-10
Map : See Map #7.
Highlights : Wickenburg.
Yarnell Hill and the Shrine of St. Joseph.
Prescott - The Capitol Building.
Prescott - Sharlot Hall Museum.
Jerome (Ghost Town).
Tuzigoot Indian Ruins.
Sedona.

Leave Phoenix on Interstate 17 - North.	
Ride approximately 20 miles to Rt. 74 West. (Exit 223)	Turn left. (Carefree Highway)
Ride 31 miles to Rt. 60.	Turn right (North).
Ride 11 miles to Wickenburg.	Turn right onto Rt. 93.
Ride 5 miles to Congress and Rt. 71.	Bear right and stay on Rt. 89. Watch for "Frog Rock" just north of Congress on the west side of the road.
Ride 9 miles to Yarnell.	
Ride 31 miles to Prescott.	Stay on Rt. 89 through town.
Ride 7 miles to Rt. 89A.	Turn right (East).
Ride 26 miles to Jerome.	
Ride 6 miles to Tuzigoot Ruins. These are some of the best Indian ruins in Arizona. These are well worth seeing.	
Ride 3 miles to Cottonwood.	
Ride 13 miles to Sedona.	
Ride 25 miles to Flagstaff.	

Day Ride : **Phoenix to Flagstaff via Payson. (162 mi)**
Hours : 6
Map : See Map #7.
Highlights : Strawberry Schoolhouse.
The bar/restaurant behind Mormon Lake.
Tonto Natural Bridge.

Leave Phoenix (Scottsdale) on Rt. 87 North.	
Ride 85 miles to Payson.	Stay on Rt. 87 North.
Ride 10 miles to the Tonto Natural Bridge.	This is worth seeing, but be very careful on the road down. Read about it in the Arizona Attractions section of this book.
Ride 5 miles to Pine.	
Ride 2 miles to Strawberry. The oldest schoolhouse in Arizona is in Strawberry. Read about it in the back of this book.	
Ride 21 miles to Clint's Well.	Turn left onto Forest Road 3 (Lake Mary Road) toward Flagstaff via Happy Jack.
Ride 11 miles to Happy Jack.	
Ride 13 miles to Mormon Lake.	Turn left and ride the loop behind Mormon Lake. There's a neat cowboy bar and restaurant back there.
Ride 15 miles to Flagstaff.	

Day Ride : **Phoenix to Las Vegas, NV. (246 mi)**
Hours : 6-8
Map : See Map #9.
Highlights : Wickenburg.
Hoover Dam.
Las Vegas.

Leave Phoenix on Interstate 17 - North.	
Ride approximately 20 miles to Rt. 74 West. (Exit 223)	Turn left. (Carefree Highway)
Ride 31 miles to Rt. 60.	Turn right (North).
Ride 11 miles to Wickenburg.	Turn right onto Rt. 93.
Ride 6 miles to Rt. 89 intersection. Stay on Rt. 93.	Bear left and stay on Rt. 93.
Be very careful on Rt. 93. It is known as "Blood Alley" for very good reason. It is a narrow, two lane road and is very heavily traveled as it is the most direct road between Phoenix and Las Vegas. Be very careful when passing other vehicles. The small white crosses on the side of the road mark the sites of fatal accidents.	
Ride 74 miles to I-40.	Turn left onto I-40 West.
Ride 26 miles to Kingman.	Turn left onto Rt. 93 North. There is a neat little side road through Chloride about 9 miles north of here. It puts you back onto Rt. 93 after Chloride.
Ride 53 miles to Hoover Dam. The tour through the dam is really neat!	
Ride 7 miles to Boulder City. See the film on the dam construction at the visitor's center.	
Ride 19 miles to Las Vegas.	

Day Ride : **Phoenix to Lake Havasu. (209 mi)**
Hours   : 6
Map   : See Map #9.
Highlights   : Wickenburg.
                 Quartzsite. Hi Jolly Monument.
                 London Bridge.

Leave Phoenix on I-17 North.	
Ride 20 miles to Rt. 74 West.	Turn left. (Carefree Highway)
Ride 31 miles to Rt. 60.	Turn right (North).
Ride 11 miles to Wickenburg.	Stay on Rt. 60.
Ride 25 miles to Aguila.	
Ride 38 miles to I-10.	Turn right onto I-10 West.
Ride 14 miles to Quartzsite.	
The Hi Jolly Monument is at the west end of town in the old cemetery. It's poorly marked and the local people don't seem to know about it. Look for a small paved road to the north. It's down the small road about a mile.	
Leave Quartzsite on Rt. 95 North.	
Ride 23 miles to Rt. 95/72.	Bear left onto Rt 95/72.
Ride 12 miles to Parker.	Turn right onto Rt. 95 North.
Ride 35 miles to Lake Havasu.	

Day Ride : **Phoenix to Sedona via Payson, Strawberry. (178 mi)**
Hours : 8
Map : See Map #7.
Highlights : Tonto Natural Bridge.
Fort Verde Historical Park.
Tuzigoot Indian Ruins.

Leave Phoenix (actually Scottsdale) on Rt. 87 North.	
Ride 85 miles to Payson.	
Ride 10 miles to the Tonto Natural Bridge.	This is worth seeing, but be very careful on the road down. Read about it in the Arizona Attractions section of this book.
Ride 5 miles to Pine.	
Ride 2 miles to Strawberry.	
Ride 16 miles to Rt. 260, the road to Camp Verde. This is known as the General Crook Highway.	Turn left (West).
Ride 33 miles to Camp Verde.	Continue straight onto Rt. 260.
Ride 14 miles to Cottonwood. Consider visiting the Tuzigoot Indian ruins. These are some of the best Indian ruins in Arizona. These are well worth seeing.	Turn right onto Rt. 89A.
Ride 13 miles to Sedona.	

Day Ride : **Phoenix to Sedona via Wickenburg, Prescott. (169 mi)**
Hours   : 8-10
Map   : See Map #7.
Highlights : Wickenburg.
               Yarnell Hill.
               Yarnell - Shrine of St. Joseph.
               Prescott - The Capitol Building.
               Prescott - Sharlot Hall Museum.
               Jerome (Ghost Town).
               Tuzigoot Indian Ruins.
               Sedona.

Leave Phoenix on Interstate 17 - North.	
Ride approximately 20 miles to Rt. 74 West. (Exit 223)	Turn left. (Carefree Highway)
Ride 31 miles to Rt. 60.	Turn right (North).
Ride 11 miles to Wickenburg.	Turn right onto Rt. 93.
Ride 6 miles to Rt. 89.	Turn right onto Rt. 89.
Ride 5 miles to Congress and Rt. 71.	Bear right and stay on Rt. 89. Watch for "Frog Rock" just north of Congress on the west side of the road.
Ride 9 miles to Yarnell.	
Ride 30 miles to Prescott.	Stay on Rt. 89 through town.
Ride 7 miles to Rt. 89A.	Turn right (East).
Ride 26 miles to Jerome.	
Ride 6 miles to Tuzigoot Ruins. These are some of the best Indian ruins in Arizona. These are well worth seeing.	
Ride 3 miles to Cottonwood.	
Ride 13 miles to Sedona.	

Day Ride : **Phoenix to Show Low via Payson. (168 mi)**
Hours : 6
Map : See Map #10.
Highlights : The Mogollon Rim.

Leave Phoenix (actually Scottsdale) on Rt. 87 North.	
Ride 85 miles to Payson.	Turn right onto Rt. 260 East.
Ride 83 miles to Show Low.	

Day Ride : **Phoenix to Show Low via Globe. (171 mi)**
Hours : 8
Map : See Map #10.
Highlights : The Salt River Canyon.

Leave Phoenix on Rt. 60/360 East.	
Ride 25 miles to Apache Junction.	Stay on Rt. 60.
Ride 16 miles to Florence Junction.	Bear left and stay on Rt. 60 East.
Ride 16 miles to Superior.	
Ride 16 miles to Miami.	
Ride 7 miles to Globe.	Turn left onto Rt. 77 North.
Ride 32 miles to Seneca Lake.	
Ride 5 miles into the Salt River Canyon.	
Ride 5 miles out of the Salt River Canyon.	
Ride 25 miles to Carrizo.	
Ride 24 miles to Show Low.	

Day Ride : **Phoenix to Tucson via Florence. (129 mi)**
Hours : 6
Map : See Map #11.
Highlights : Florence - Prison Museum.
Florence - McFarland Historical State Park.
Oracle Junction - Biosphere II.
Mission San Xavier del Bac

Leave Phoenix on Rt. 60 East.	
Ride 25 miles to Apache Junction. The freeway ends but the road continues as a smaller highway. The number (Rt. 60) stays the same.	Stay on Rt. 60.
Ride 16 miles to Florence Junction.	Bear right on Rt. 79.
Ride 17 miles to Florence. The little museum at the south end of town has a neat collection of used hangmans nooses.	
Ride 42 miles to Oracle Junction. Consider seeing Biosphere II.	Bear right onto Rt. 77. (South)
Ride 28 miles to Tucson.	

Mission San Xavier del Bac, an unforgettable experience!

(Photo by author)

Day Ride : **Phoenix to Williams via Rt. 89. (184 mi)**
Hours : 6
Map : See Maps #7 & #9.
Highlights : Wickenburg.
Yarnell Hill.
Yarnell - Shrine of St. Joseph.
Prescott - The Capitol Building.
Prescott - Sharlot Hall Museum.

Leave Phoenix on Interstate 17 - North.	
Ride approximately 20 miles to Rt. 74 West. (Exit 223)	Turn left. (Carefree Highway)
Ride 31 miles to Rt. 60.	Turn right (North).
Ride 11 miles to Wickenburg.	Turn right on Rt. 93.
Ride 5 miles Rt. 89.	Turn right onto Rt. 89.
Ride 10 miles to Congress and Rt. 71.	Bear right and stay on Rt. 89. Watch for "Frog Rock" just north of Congress on the west side of the road.
Ride 9 miles to Yarnell.	
Ride 31 miles to Prescott.	Stay on Rt. 89 through town.
Ride 7 miles to Granite Dells.	Bear left and stay on Rt. 89.
Ride 11 miles to Chino Valley.	
Ride 34 miles to Interstate 40.	Turn right (East).
Ride 15 miles to Williams.	

Day Ride : **Phoenix to Yuma via Wickenburg. (222 mi)**
Hours   : 8
Map   : See Map #9.
Highlights : Wickenburg.
             Quartzsite. Hi Jolly Monument.
             Yuma. Historic Territorial Prison.

Leave Phoenix on I-17 North.	
Ride approximately 20 miles to Rt. 74 West. (Exit 223)	Turn left. (Carefree Highway)
Ride 31 miles to Rt. 60.	Turn right (North).
Ride 11 miles to Wickenburg.	Stay on Rt. 60 West.
Ride 25 miles to Aguila.	
Ride 38 miles to I-10.	Turn right onto I-10 West.
Ride 14 miles to Quartzsite.	
The Hi Jolly Monument is at the west end of town in the old cemetery. It's poorly marked and the local people don't seem to know about it. Look for a small paved road to the north. It's down the small road about a mile.	
Leave Quartzsite on Rt. 95 South.	
Ride 83 miles to Yuma.	
Visit the Yuma Territorial Prison. It's fascinating.	

Day Ride : **Phoenix to Yuma via Gila Bend. (177 mi)**
Hours   : 5
Map   : See Map #9.
Highlights : Historic Yuma Territorial Prison.
               COC-Tourist Info Center Museum in Gila Bend
               Painted Rocks (Hieroglyphics) just west of Gila Bend.

Leave Phoenix on I-10 West.	
Ride 4 miles (Approx) to Rt. 85.	Turn left onto Rt. 85 South.
Ride 32 miles to Buckeye.	Stay on Rt. 85 South.
Ride 33 miles to Gila Bend.	Turn left onto I-8 West.
Ride 50 miles to Dateland.	
Ride 13 miles to Mohawk.	
Ride 45 miles to Yuma.	

Day Ride : **Sedona to the Grand Canyon. (94 mi)**
Hours   : 3-4
Map   : See Map #12.
Highlights : Flagstaff.
               Kaibab National Forest.
               The Grand Canyon.

Leave Sedona on Rt. 89A North.
Ride 18 miles to Flagstaff.
Ride through Flagstaff. The road goes under a railroad bridge. Right after the railrad bridge watch for small signs indicating Rt. 180 turns left to the Grand Canyon. There are gas stations after the turn off.
Leave Flagstaff on Rt. 180 North.
Ride 42 miles to Valle. Stay on Rt. 180.
Ride 31 miles to Tusayan.
Ride 3 miles to the Grand Canyon.

Day Ride : Sedona to Chinle (Canyon de Chelly) (210 mi).
Hours : 8
Map : See Map #13.
Highlights : The Ride.
Canyon de Chelly.
Cautions : Call ahead. Accommodations are limited.
Call ahead for Truck Tour of Canyon de Chelly.

Leave Sedona on Rt. 89A North.	
Ride 18 miles to Interstate 40 East.	
Ride 9 miles to Exit 207, Indian Rt. 15.	Turn left (North/East) onto Indian Rt. 15.
Ride 63 miles to Rt. 87.	Turn left (North).
Ride 31 miles to Second Mesa.	Turn right (East) onto Rt. 264.
Ride 58 miles to Rt. 191.	Turn left (North).
Ride 31 miles to Chinle.	
Check into a motel and make a reservation to tour Canyon De Chelly the next morning.	

Sedona's Red Rock Country and the Chapel of the Holy Cross
(Photo courtesy Arizona Office of Tourism)

Day Ride : **Show Low to Eagar (Petrified Forest). (193 mi)**
Hours : 8
Map : See Map #3.
Highlights : The Petrified Forest.

Leave Show Low on Rt. 60 East/North.	
Ride 11 miles to connect with Rt. 61.	Bear left onto Rt. 61.
Ride 19 miles to Concho.	Bear left onto Rt. 180A.
Ride 25 miles to Woodruff. Enter the Petrified Forest National Park.	
Ride 26 miles through the Park to I-40.	Turn left (East).
Ride 28 miles to Exit 339, Sanders.	Turn right onto Rt. 191 (South).
Ride 52 miles to St. Johns.	
Ride 30 miles to Springerville.	
Ride 2 miles to Eagar.	

Map #3
Not to scale

Day Ride : **Show Low to Phoenix via Globe. (171 mi).**
Hours   : 6
Map   : See Map #10.
Highlights : The Salt River Canyon.

Leave Show Low on Rt. 60 South.	
Ride 24 miles to Carrizo.	
Ride 25 miles to the Salt River Canyon.	
Ride 5 miles to the bottom of the Salt River Canyon.	
Ride 5 miles to the top of the Salt River Canyon.	
Ride 32 miles to Globe.	Turn right onto Rt. 60.
Ride 7 miles to Miami.	
Ride 16 miles to Superior.	
Ride 16 miles to Florence Junction.	Stay to the right on Rt. 60.
Ride 16 miles to Apache Junction. Here the small Rt.60 connects to the large Rt.60.	
Ride 25 miles to Phoenix.	

Day Ride : **Show Low to Phoenix via Payson. (168 mi)**
Hours   : 6
Map   : See Map #10.
Highlights : The Mogollon Rim.

Leave Show Low on Rt. 260 West.	
Ride 83 miles to Payson.	Turn left onto Rt. 87 South.
Ride 85 miles to Phoenix.	

Day Ride : **Show Low to Tucson. (203 mi)**
Hours   :   8
Map   :   See Map #6.
Highlights :   The Salt River Canyon.

Leave Show Low on Rt. 60 South.	
Ride 24 miles to Carrizo.	
Ride 25 miles to the Salt River Canyon.	
Ride 5 miles to the bottom of the Salt River Canyon.	
Ride 5 miles to the top of the Salt River Canyon.	
Ride 3 miles to Seneca.	
Ride 32 miles to Globe.	Turn left onto Rt. 70 East.
Ride 1 mile and turn right onto Rt. 77 South.	
Ride 30 miles to Christmas.	
Ride 9 miles to Winkelman.	
Ride 19 miles to Mammoth.	
Ride 22 miles to Oracle Junction. Consider seeing Biosphere II.	Bear left and stay on Rt. 77.
Ride 28 miles to Tucson.	

Day Ride : **Show Low to Willcox via Globe. (191 mi)**
Hours : **8**
Map : See Map #6.
Highlights : The Salt River Canyon.

Leave Show Low on Rt. 60 South.	
Ride 24 miles to Carrizo.	
Ride 25 miles to the Salt River Canyon.	
Ride 5 miles to the bottom of the Salt River Canyon.	
Ride 5 miles to the top of the Salt River Canyon.	
Ride 32 miles to Globe.	Turn left onto Rt. 70 East.
Ride 55 miles to Safford.	Turn right onto Rt. 191 South.
Ride 33 miles to I-10.	Turn right onto I-10 West.
Ride 12 miles to Willcox.	

Map #6
Not to scale

Day Ride : **Show Low to Willcox via Rt. 191. (260 mi)**
Hours   : 8
Map   : See Map #6.
Highlights : Rt. 191 is spectacular.

Leave Show Low on Rt. 60/260 East.	
Ride 58 miles to Eagar.	Turn right onto Rt. 180/191 (South)
Ride 27 miles to Alpine.	
Ride 83 miles to Morenci.	
Ride 7 miles to Clifton.	
Ride 9 miles to Threeway.	Turn right onto Rt. 191 (West).
Ride 24 miles to Rt. 70.	Turn right onto Rt. 70.
Ride 7 miles to Safford.	Turn left onto Rt. 191.
Ride 33 miles to I-10.	Turn right onto I-10 West.
Ride 12 miles to Willcox.	

Day Ride : **Tucson to Bisbee via Tombstone. (112 mi)**
Hours   : 5
Map   : See Map #1.
Highlights : Tombstone.
               Bisbee.
               Copper Queen Mine.

Leave Tucson on I-10 East.	
Ride 22 miles to Rt. 83.	Turn right onto Rt. 83 South.
Ride 27 miles to Sonoita.	Turn left onto Rt. 82 East.
Ride 36 miles to Rt. 80.	Turn right onto Rt. 80 South.
Ride 3 miles to Tombstone.	
Ride 24 miles to Bisbee.	

Day Ride : **Tucson to Phoenix via Florence. (128 mi)**
Hours   : 5
Map   : See Map #11.
Highlights : Florence Museum.

Leave Tucson on Rt. 77/79 North.	
Ride 28 miles to Oracle Junction. Consider seeing Biosphere II.	Turn left onto Rt. 79 North.
Ride 42 miles to Florence. The little museum at the south end of town has a neat collection of used hangmans nooses.	
Ride 17 miles to Rt. 60.	Turn left onto Rt. 60.
Ride 16 miles to Apache Junction. The small Rt. 60 becomes large Rt. 60.	Stay on Rt. 60 West.
Ride 20 miles (Approx) to Phoenix.	

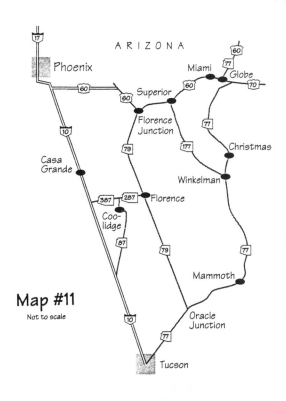

Map #11
Not to scale

Day Ride : **Tucson to Phoenix via Globe. (192 mi)**
Hours   : 6
Map   : See Map #11.
Highlights : The ride.

Leave Tucson on Rt. 77/79 North.	
Ride 28 miles to Oracle Junction. Consider seeing Biosphere II.	Turn right onto Rt. 77 East.
Ride 22 miles to Mammoth.	
Ride 21 miles to Winkelman.	Turn right onto Rt. 77 North/East.
Ride 9 miles to Christmas.	
Ride 30 miles to intersect with Rt. 70.	Turn left (West).
Ride 2 miles to Globe. Rt. 70 becomes Rt. 60.	
Ride 7 miles to Miami.	
Ride 16 miles to Superior.	
Ride 16 miles to Florence Junction.	Bear right onto Rt. 60.
Ride 16 miles to Apache Junction. Here the small Rt. 60 becomes large Rt. 60.	
Ride 25 miles (Approx) to Phoenix.	

Day Ride : Tucson to Yuma. (294 mi)
Hours   : 6-8
Map   : See Map #14.
Highlights : Historic Yuma Territorial Prison.
                 COC-Tourist Info Center Museum in Gila Bend
                 Painted Rocks (Hieroglyphics) just west of Gila Bend.

Leave Tucson on Rt. 86 West.	
Ride 38 miles to Kitt Peak Road (Rt. 386).	
Ride 9 miles up to Kitt Peak.	
Ride 9 miles down from Kitt Peak.	Turn left onto Rt. 86.
Ride 46 miles to Quijotoa.	
Ride 31 miles to Rt. 85.	Turn right onto Rt. 85 North.
Ride 10 miles to Ajo. Pronounced "Ah-ho".	
Ride 43 miles to Gila Bend.	Turn left onto I-8 West.
Ride 50 miles to Dateland.	
Ride 13 miles to Mohawk.	
Ride 45 miles to Yuma.	

Map #14
Not to scale

Day Ride : Willcox to Bisbee. (200 mi)
Hours : 8
Map : See Map #1.
Highlights : Dos Cabezas (Ghost Town).
Amerind Foundation.
Chiricahua National Monument.
Bisbee.

Leave Willcox on Rt. 186 South.	
Ride 15 miles to Dos Cabezas.	
Ride 17 miles to the Chiricahua National Monument.	Turn left.
Ride 11 miles into Chiricahua National Monument.	
Ride 11 miles out of Chiricahua National Monument.	
Leave the Chiricahua National Monument on Rt. 181 South.	
Ride 23 miles to intersect with Rt. 191.	Turn right (North).
Ride 18 miles to the road to Dragoon.	Turn left (West).
Ride 10 miles to Dragoon.	
Ride 2 miles to the Amerind Foundation. This foundation displays the finest collection of Indian artifacts in Arizona.	
Leave the Amerind Foundation and head back to Dragoon.	
Ride 2 miles back to Dragoon.	
Ride 10 miles back to Rt. 191.	Turn right onto Rt. 191 (South).
Ride 18 miles back to the Rt. 181 intersection.	Stay on 191.
Ride 38 miles to Douglas.	Turn right onto Rt. 80 West.
Ride 25 miles to Bisbee.	
If there is still daylight left, ride 24 miles north and enjoy Tombstone. Then return to Bisbee.	

Day Ride : **Willcox to Eagar via Rt. 191. (202 mi)**
Hours　　 : 6
Map　　　 : See Map #6.
Highlights : Rt. 191.

Leave Willcox on I-10 East.	
Ride 12 miles to Rt. 191.	Turn left onto Rt. 191 North.
Ride 33 miles to Safford.	Turn right onto Rt. 70 East.
Ride 7 miles to Rt. 191.	Turn left onto Rt. 191 North.
Ride 24 miles to Threeway.	Turn left onto Rt. 191 North.
Ride 9 miles to Clifton.	
Ride 7 miles to Morenci.	
Ride 83 miles to Alpine.	Turn left onto Rt. 180 North.
Ride 27 miles to Eagar.	

Day Ride : **Willcox to Show Low via Globe. (191 mi)**
Hours　　 : 6
Map　　　 : See Map #6.
Highlights : The Salt River Canyon.

Leave Willcox on I-10 East.	
Ride 12 miles to Rt. 191.	Turn left onto Rt. 191 North.
Ride 33 miles to Safford.	Turn left on Rt. 70 West.
Ride 55 miles to Globe.	Turn right onto Rt. 77 North.
Ride 32 miles to Seneca.	
Ride 5 miles into the Salt River Canyon.	
Ride 5 miles out of the Salt River Canyon.	
Ride 25 miles to Carrizo.	
Ride 24 miles to Show Low.	

Day Ride : **Willcox to Show Low via Rt. 191. (260 mi)**
Hours   : 8
Map   : See Map #6.
Highlights : Rt. 191 is spectacular.

Leave Willcox on I-10 East.	
Ride 12 miles to Rt. 191.	Turn left onto Rt. 191 North.
Ride 33 miles to Safford.	Turn right onto Rt. 70 East.
Ride 7 miles to Rt. 191.	Turn left onto Rt. 191.
Ride 24 miles to Threeway.	Turn left onto Rt. 191 North.
Ride 9 miles to Clifton.	
Ride 7 miles to Morenci.	
Ride 83 miles to Alpine.	
Ride 27 miles to Eagar.	Turn left onto Rt. 260.
Ride 58 miles to Show Low.	

Map #6
Not to scale

Day Ride : **Willcox to Tucson. Scenic Route (224 mi)**
Hours : 8-10
Map : See Map #1.
Highlights : Dos Cabezas (Ghost Town).
Chiricahua National Monument.
Bisbee.
Tombstone.

Leave Willcox on Rt. 186 South.	
Ride 9 miles to Dos Cabezas.	
Ride 23 miles to the Chiricahua National Monument. Go into the Chiricahua Monument. It is well worth seeing. When you leave the monument turn left (South) onto Rt. 181.	
Ride 23 miles on Rt. 181 to intersect with Rt. 191.	Turn left (South) onto Rt. 191.
Ride 38 miles to Douglas.	Turn right onto Rt. 80 West.
Ride 23 miles to Bisbee.	
Ride 24 miles to Tombstone.	
Ride 3 miles to intersect with Rt. 82.	Turn left (West).
Ride 32 miles to Sonoita.	Turn right (North) onto Rt. 83.
Ride 27 miles to I-10.	Turn left (West) onto I-10.
Ride 22 miles to Tucson.	

Day Ride : Williams to Grand Canyon and Return. (122 mi)
Hours   : 8-10
Map   : See Map #12.
Highlights : The Grand Canyon.

Leave Williams on I-40 East.	
Ride 2 miles to Rt. 64.	Turn left onto Rt. 64 North.
Ride 28 miles to Valle.	
Ride 31 miles to the Grand Canyon.	
Enjoy the Grand Canyon.	Ride or take the shuttle out to the end and see Hermit's Rest.
Ride the 26 mile scenic ride on Rt. 64 from the Grand Canyon to Desert View, and return to the Grand Canyon. The first two overlooks are the best for "me and my bike at the Grand Canyon photos."	
Return to Tusayan and see the IMAX Theater Grand Canyon movie.	
Leave the Grand Canyon on Rt. 64 South.	
Ride 31 miles to Valle.	
Ride 28 miles to I-40.	Turn right onto I-40 West.
Ride 2 miles to Williams.	

Day Ride : **Williams to Las Vegas, NV. (227 mi)**
Hours   : 7-8
Map   : See Map #9.
Highlights : The last section of Historic Rt. 66.
           Hoover Dam.
           Las Vegas.

Leave Williams on I-40 West.	
Ride 22 miles (Approx) to Exit 139.	Exit onto Rt. 66.
Ride 19 miles to Seligman.	
Ride 51 miles to Valentine.	
Ride 32 miles to I-40.	Turn right onto I-40 West.
Ride 7 miles to Rt.93.	Turn right onto Rt. 93 North/West.
Ride 70 miles to Hoover Dam. The tour through the dam is really neat.	
Ride 7 miles to Boulder City. See the movie on the dam construction at the visitor's center.	
Ride 19 miles to Las Vegas.	

Day Ride : **Williams to Phoenix via Flagstaff/Sedona. (230 mi)**
Hours : 10
Map : See Map #7.
Highlights : Oak Creek.
Sedona.
Tuzigoot (Indian Ruins).
Jerome (Ghost Town).
Prescott.
Yarnell Hill.
Wickenburg.

Leave Williams on I-40 East.	
Ride 31 miles to Flagstaff.	Turn right onto Rt. 89A (South).
Ride 25 miles to Oak Creek/Sedona.	Stay on Rt. 89A.
Ride 13 miles to Cottonwood.	
Ride 6 miles to Tuzigoot Indian Ruins. These are some of the best Indian ruins in Arizona. These are well worth seeing.	
Ride 6 miles to Jerome. Spend a couple of hours here.	
Ride 26 miles to Granite Dells.	Turn left onto Rt. 89 South/West.
Ride 7 miles to Prescott.	Ride through Prescott on Rt. 89.
Ride 31 miles to Yarnell.	
Ride 9 miles to Congress.	Bear left and stay on Rt. 89. Watch for "Frog Rock" just north of Congress.
Ride 10 miles to Rt. 93.	Turn left onto Rt. 93.
Ride 5 miles to Wickenburg.	
Ride 11 miles to Rt. 74.	Turn left onto Rt. 74.
Ride 31 miles to I-17.	Turn right onto I-17 South.
Ride 20 miles to Phoenix.	

Day Ride : **Williams to Phoenix via Rt. 89. (184 mi)**
Hours   : 6
Map   : See Map #7.
Highlights : Prescott.
                Yarnell Hill.
                Wickenburg.

Leave Williams on I-40 West.	
Ride 15 miles to Ash Fork and Rt 89.	Turn left onto Rt. 89 (South).
Ride 34 miles to Chino Valley.	
Ride 11 miles to Granite Dells.	Stay on Rt. 89.
Ride 7 miles to Prescott.	Ride through Prescott on Rt. 89.
Ride 31 miles to Yarnell.	
Ride 9 miles to Congress and Rt. 71.	Bear left and stay on Rt. 89. Watch for "Frog Rock" just north of Congress on the west side of the road.
Ride 10 miles to Rt. 93.	Turn left onto Rt. 93.
Ride 6 miles to Wickenburg.	
Ride 11 miles to Rt. 74.	Turn left onto Rt. 74.
Ride 31 miles to I-17.	Turn right onto I-17 South.
Ride approximately 20 miles to Phoenix.	

Day Ride : **Yuma to Lake Havasu. (153 mi)**
Hours : 4
Map : See Map #9.
Highlights : Historic Yuma Territorial Prison.
The Grave of Hi Jolly.
London Bridge.

Leave Yuma on Rt. 95 North.	
Ride 83 miles to Quartzsite.	
The Hi Jolly Monument is at the west end of town in the old cemetery. It's poorly marked and the local people don't seem to know about it. Look for a small paved road to the north. It's down the small road about a mile.	
Ride 23 miles to Rt. 72.	Turn left (merge) onto Rt. 72.
Ride 12 miles to Parker.	
Ride 35 miles to Lake Havasu.	

Day Ride : **Yuma to Phoenix via Gila Bend. (177 mi)**
Hours : 6
Map : See Map #9.
Highlights : Historic Yuma Territorial Prison.
COC-Tourist Info Center Museum in Gila Bend
Painted Rocks (Hieroglyphics) just west of Gila Bend.

Leave Yuma on I-8 East.	
Ride 19 miles to Exit 21.	Exit onto the small road which runs next to I-8.
Ride 26 miles to Mohawk.	Enter I-8 East again.
Ride 13 miles to Dateland.	
Ride 50 miles to Gila bend.	Turn left onto Rt. 85 North.
Ride 38 miles to I-10.	Turn right (East) onto I-10.
Ride 36 miles to Phoenix.	

Day Ride : **Yuma to Tucson. (294 mi)**
Hours   : 8-10
Map   : See Map #14.
Highlights : Historic Yuma Territorial Prison.
             COC-Tourist Info Center Museum in Gila Bend
             Painted Rocks (Hieroglyphics) just west of Gila Bend.
             Organ Pipe National Monument.
             Kitt Peak Observatory.

Leave Yuma on I-8 East.	
Ride 19 miles to Exit 21.	Exit onto the small road which runs next to I-8.
Ride 26 miles to Mohawk.	Enter I-8 East again.
Ride 13 miles to Dateland.	
Ride 50 miles to Gila Bend.	Turn right onto Rt. 85 South.
Ride 43 miles to Ajo. (Pronounce "Ah-ho")	
Ride 10 miles to connect with Rt. 86.	Bear left onto Rt. 86.

Alternative
Stay on Rt. 85. Ride 21 miles into Organ Pipe National Monument. It is beautiful and has a nice visitor's center. When you leave, ride 21 miles north and turn right onto Rt. 86 (East).

Ride 31 miles to Quijotoa.	
Ride 46 miles to Kitt Peak. Turn left onto Rt. 386.	Ride 9 miles up Kitt Peak.
Ride 9 miles down Kitt Peak. (Yes, it's worth it.)	
Turn right and ride 38 miles to Tucson.	

Trains! Trains! Trains!

I love trains. Especially old trains. Here are three of the best. Please consider taking a day off from riding to relax and let an iron horse take you through some great Southwest scenery.

Cottonwood, AZ.

This is a very nice half day train ride in and out of some beautiful Arizona back country. It's very relaxing and low key. This historic railroad used to connect the mining town of Jerome to the state capital, Prescott. Call 602-639-0010.

Williams, AZ.

Ride a steam train from Williams to the Grand Canyon and back. The scenery is spectacular! This is a nice way to take a day off from riding and still see some beautiful mountain scenery. Call 1-800-843-8724.

Durango, CO.

Ride the most incredible train ride of your life. This unbelievable steam train runs from Durango to Silverton and back. The first time I rode it I shot three rolls of 36 exposure film! And I would have shot more if I'd had it. Call 303-247-2733.

Phoenix Area Day Rides.

The next few pages contain some nice day rides out of and returning to Phoenix for those folks who are visiting Phoenix and don't have time to go on an extended tour.

All the miles listed here are approximate and depend on your starting point and how much you like to meander. The times are also approximate and depend on whether you want to stop, look, and actually enjoy what you are riding through, or just rack up the miles.

Day Ride 1 - Phoenix to Bartlett Lake and Return.

Go North from Phoenix on Cave Creek Road or Scottsdale Road. Either one will take you to the towns of Cave Creek and Carefree. These two roads come together in Cave Creek. Have a nice meal at the Horny Toad or the Satisfied Frog. Eating at "The Toad" is worthwhile just to learn how it got it's name. However, "The Frog" is larger (and has a non-smoking section) and you may get seated faster. While in Cave Creek you might consider seeing the Cave Creek Museum (602-488-2764). It's unique in that almost all of the displays consist of items from the local area. The Indian artifacts fill a whole wing and there's a very nice exhibit of mining tools. After the museum ride East on Cave Creek road past the Scottsdale Road turn off and follow the signs to Bartlett Lake. It's a beautiful ride. Time: 4-6 Hours. Miles: 70

Day Ride 2 - Phoenix to Roosevelt Lake and Return.

Ride North on Rt. 87 toward Payson but turn right onto Rt. 188. Ride through Punkin (yes, that's spelled right) Center. There is a small cafe in Punkin Center on top of a hill to the left at the fork in the road. Continue East on 188 to Roosevelt Lake. Stop and check out the reconstruction of the dam. It's quite an effort. Do NOT turn onto the Apache Trail! It's 35 miles of loose dirt and gravel. Stay on the pavement and continue West on Rt. 188 to Globe. Turn right onto Rt. 60 and ride one of the most scenic high speed roads in Arizona. It's a great ride to Florence Junction. Then follow Rt. 60 back to Mesa and on to Phoenix. Time 8 hours. Miles: 225.

Day Ride 3 - Phoenix to Tortilla Flat and Return.

Head South from Phoenix and turn east onto Rt. 60, The Superstition Freeway. Ride about 20 miles to Apache Junction and turn left (North) onto Rt.88. Ride about 23 miles to Tortilla Flat. When the pavement ends you're there. This is a "world famous" motorcyclist gathering place. The Arizona equivalent of The Rock Store. Don't go down the Apache Trail. It's 35 miles of dirt and gravel. It's hot, dusty, and dangerous. It's just not worth it. Time 4-6 hours. Miles: 70

Day Ride 4 - Rawhide and Pioneer Living History Museum.

Let's face it. Rawhide is a tourist trap. But it's a fun tourist trap. It's a complete old western town built the way Hollywood would if Hollywood could. If you are hungry, pass up Rawhide and ride out to Pinnacle Peak Restaurant. It is a tourist trap also, but the food is average and the gun fighters are friendly. To get there:

- Ride north from Rawhide to Pinnacle Peak Road. Turn right onto Pinnacle Peak Road.
- Ride to Pima Road. Turn left onto Pima.
- Ride to Happy Valley Road. Turn right onto Happy Valley.
- Ride to Alma School Road. Turn left onto Alma School.

If you want something more real, go past Pinnacle Peak Restaurant to Riata Pass as that's where the locals eat. If you want something even more real, stop at Greasewood Flats (but be careful on the dirt road in). This is an authentic old western, locals only, cowboy/biker bar. There is no fakery here, this is the real west, warts and all. After you eat ride back to Rawhide and see how Hollywood would have done it.

After leaving Rawhide, ride a little farther north on Scottsdale Road to the Carefree Highway, turn left and ride to Interstate 17. Turn right and ride about 2 to 3 miles north on Interstate 17 and you come to the old western town of Pioneer Arizona. This is a complete reconstruction made of over 20 original buildings gathered from all over Arizona. They are open during the cooler months only so call first if you're here during the summer. Hours are 9AM to 5PM. Admission is $5.75. The telephone number is 993-0212. Time 6+ hours. Miles: 100

Day Ride 5 - Phoenix to Prescott and Return.

Ride 20 miles North on Interstate 17 to the Carefree Highway. Turn left and ride to Wickenburg. (Stop at the Lake Pleasant overlook, it's a great view.) Have a nice breakfast or lunch at the Gold Nugget. (Park behind it and enter through the back entrance.) When you leave the Gold Nugget, ride toward the stoplight and pull into the Circle K convenience store parking lot. Get a photo of the "Jail Tree". It served as the town jail from 1863 to 1890. Turn right onto Rt. 93 and then 6 miles later, right onto Rt.89 and ride to Yarnell, and Prescott. See the Sharlot Hall Museum. Return to Phoenix on I-17. This is a great, full, day ride. Time 6 to 8 hours. Miles: 228.

Day Ride 6 - Wickenburg and the Vulture Mine.

Ride 20 miles North on Interstate 17 to the Carefree Highway. Turn left and ride to Wickenburg. (Stop at the Lake Pleasant overlook, it's a great view.) Have a nice breakfast or lunch at the Gold Nugget. (Park behind it and enter through the back entrance.) When you leave the Nugget ride toward the stoplight and pull into the Circle K convenience store parking lot. Look behind the Circle K and get a photo of the "Jail Tree". It served as the town jail from 1863 to 1890.

Continue west on Rt. 60 2 miles to the Vulture Mine turn off. Turn left (South) and ride 13 miles to the mine. It's all paved except for the entrance to the parking lot. The Vulture Mine was started by Henry Wickenburg. The story is he bent over to pick up a vulture he had shot and saw the ground was laced with gold. The Vulture Mine is closed now, but the old buildings and machinery are still standing. It's privately owned and admission is inexpensive. The walking tour of the area is self guided and can be hot in the summer months. Bring a hat and carry water. Be sure to get a photo of the hanging tree. Henry Wickenburg hung 18 men from that tree. He was a tough boss. Time 6+ hours. Miles 130.

Day Ride 7 - Phoenix to Payson and Return.

Ride North on Rt. 87 to Payson.   Consider seeing the Tonto Natural Bridge, but be very careful. The ride downhill to the bridge is 3 miles of loose dirt and gravel. (The road is scheduled for paving in late 1994. Yea!!) Ride North to Pine and Strawberry. See the oldest schoolhouse in Arizona (described below).   Ride North to the turn off   to Cordes Junction. Turn left (West) and ride one of the nicest roads in Arizona to I-17. Turn left (South) and return to Phoenix. This is a great day ride. Time 8 hours. Miles: 250.

Day Ride 8 - Phoenix to Florence, Casa Grande, and Return.

Ride East on Rt. 60 to Florence Junction. Turn right (South) and ride to Florence.   See the museum in Florence. It has a neat collection of used hangman's nooses with pictures of the "usees" in them. Ride West out of Florence on Rt. 287 and stop at the Casa Grande (Big House) Indian ruins. Continue West on Rt. 287 to Rt. 87/287 bear right (North). Follow Rt. 87/287 to Rt. 87 North through Chandler and back to Phoenix. Hours: 4-6. Miles: 150.

Gravestone of Charles A. Hamblin — on the Coronado Trail

(see story page 121 - Photo by author)

The "pincushion tree" on the Coronado Trail

(see story page 121 - Photo by author)

Arizona Attractions.

There are hundreds of interesting things to do and places to see in Arizona. For convenience, the following attractions are listed as being in the North, Central, East, West, or Southern part of the state.

Central Arizona Attractions.

Central - Apache Trail.

I'm listing the Apache Trail because it's well known and seems to be high on visitor's "must see" lists. But I'm not recommending it to you. It is pretty, yes. It is spectacular, maybe. It is 35 miles of narrow dirt road, absolutely. Dusty, narrow, no room to pass, loose gravel and dirt road. It can be ridden, but it's not fun.

The biggest reason to stay off the Apache Trail is it is heavily traveled by RV'ers heading for Roosevelt Lake. So you'll find yourself following an RV towing a boat, and being followed (tailgated) by another RV towing a boat. You'll feel like a piece of meat in a sandwich. I'll wait until they pave the darn thing before I ride it again.

If you want to visit Roosevelt Lake, ride up Rt. 87 to Rt. 188 (Jakes Corner), turn right and ride through Punkin Center. When you leave the dam, continue south to Globe. It's a great day ride from Phoenix!

Central - Camp Verde. Indian Ruins.

Near Camp Verde are two of the best Indian ruins in Arizona. Montezuma's Castle and Tuzigoot ruins. Tuzigoot is smaller but you get to walk right into the old ruins and even go inside a room. I like Tuzigoot better.

Tuzigoot ruins are 10 miles west of Camp Verde on Route 260. Turn off I-17 at Route 260 and head towards Cottonwood. Turn west onto Route 89 and ride to Clarkdale. Follow the signs to the Tuzigoot Ruins National Monument.

Montezuma's Castle is just north of Camp Verde on I-17 at Exit 293, and is the more visually impressive of the two, but all you can do is look at it. You can't really get near it.

Central - Camp Verde. Fort Verde Historical Park.

In Camp Verde, consider visiting the Fort Verde Historical Park. It's a restored frontier fort and has a nice museum. It is well presented and it doesn't take a lot of time to enjoy it all.

Central - Phoenix. The Arizona Museum.

Located at 10th Avenue and Van Buren this museum boasts a collection of mining equipment (including two steam locomotives) and of particular interest to motorcyclists, a steam engine which powered one of the earliest motorcycles.

Central - Phoenix. The Old State Capitol Building.

The original Capitol Building was built in 1900, twelve years before Arizona became a state. It served us well and is now maintained as a museum. It's located at 3rd avenue and Washington Street. There are a lot of nice displays. The park in front has the anchor and signal mast from the Battleship USS Arizona, which was sunk at Pearl Harbor.

Central - Phoenix. Heritage Square.

The Rosson House is the centerpiece of this eclectic combination of old and new. The house dates back to the 1890's and has been restored to its original grandeur. It is surrounded by other houses which were moved to the square from around Phoenix. The Lath House Pavilion is the modern focal point and it nicely complements the old houses. Everything is open for tours. Costs are minimal.

Central - Phoenix. Pioneer Living History Museum.

Ride about 22 miles directly north on Interstate 17 and you come to the old western town of Pioneer Arizona. It's just north of the Carefree Highway (Rt.74). This is a complete reconstruction made of over 20 original buildings gathered from all over Arizona. They are open during the cooler months only so call first if you're here during the Summer. Hours are 9AM to 5PM. Admission is $5.75. The telephone number is 993-0212.

Central - Phoenix. The Mystery Castle.

Strange, strange, strange. Arizona seems to attract strange people. No one knows why Mr. Boyce Gully built the mystery castle, but he did. And he used everything from native mud to old auto parts. It stands at Mineral Road and 7th Street just before the entrance to South Mountain Park. There's a nominal fee, but it's worth it. After touring the Castle take a ride through South Mountain Park.

Central - Phoenix. The Hall of Flame.

This fascinating museum holds over 100 fully restored fire engines and vehicles. It has over 30,000 square feet of floor space containing hundreds of fire fighting exhibits, and is known as the largest fire fighting museum in the world. The Hall of Flame is sponsored by the National Historical Fire Foundation. The museum is located at 6101 East Van Buren Street across from the Phoenix Zoo, the hours are 9AM to 5PM Monday through Saturday, and admission is $3.00.

Central - Phoenix. Rawhide Arizona.

Let's face it. Rawhide is a tourist trap. But it's a fun tourist trap. It's a complete old western town built the way Hollywood would if Hollywood could. If you are hungry, pass up Rawhide and ride out to Pinnacle Peak Restaurant. It is also a tourist trap, but the food is average and the gun fighters are friendly. To get there:

- Ride north from Rawhide and turn right (East) onto Pinnacle Peak Road.
- Ride to Pima Road. Turn left onto Pima.
- Ride to Happy Valley Road. Turn right onto Happy Valley.
- Ride to Alma School Road. Turn left onto Alma School.

If you want something more real, go past Pinnacle Peak to Riata Pass as that's where the locals eat. If you want something even more real, stop at Greasewood Flats (but be careful on the dirt road in). This is an authentic old western, locals only, cowboy/biker bar. There is no fakery here, this is the real west, warts and all. After you eat ride back to Rawhide and see how Hollywood would have done it.

Northern Arizona Attractions.

North - Chinle. Canyon De Chelly.

Canyon De Chelly (pronounced "Canyon d' Shay") is beautiful! There is also a lot of history to be learned there. Pay attention and you'll learn why the famous Kit Carson is not a local hero. You can look into the canyon from roads along both sides, but the only way to go into the canyon is in half or full day six-wheel truck tour run by the local Indians. Both are very interesting tours and well worth doing.

Take the truck tour through Canyon de Chelly and see some of the oldest Hohokam Indian ruins in Arizona. White House Ruin is magnificent! Then ride along the rim of the canyon and see Spider Rock, the towering spire featured in the movie Poltergeist II.

Leaving Chinle, visit the **Hubbell Trading Post**. This is a real trading post! Not a tourist attraction. It is the oldest continually operating Indian trading post in America.

North - Four Corners.

Located in the northeast corner of Arizona, "Four Corners" is the only place in the United States where you can stand in four states at one time. For years it was neglected and was just a rather drab spot near the road. Now it has been fixed up and the local Native Americans have set up small business selling jewelry, blankets, and other souvenirs. There is a small admission charge, but it is worth it.

North - Grand Canyon. The North Rim.

The North Rim of the Grand Canyon is 210 miles away from the South Rim. Ten miles across and 200 miles around. It's a heck of a ride from the South Rim to the North Rim, some of it dreary, most of it beautiful, and the destination is well worth it if you have the time to spend.

Putting it bluntly, the North Rim of the Grand Canyon is more beautiful than the South Rim, and being a lot harder to get to it's much less crowded. This, to me, makes it much more enjoyable. The difference in beauty is in the topography. The South Rim is in "High Desert" country, while the North Rim is 8200 feet up in "Tall Pines" country. The difference is total.

There are only a few places to stay while at the North Rim. The National

Parks Service has cabins right at the North Rim, but they fill up fast and are usually booked months in advance by people who live to plan ahead.

The next nearest place is Kaibab Lodge. This is a nice, but small, establishment. Jacob Lake has cabins and rooms available, and that will probably be the best place to get a room on short notice.

North - Grand Canyon. The South Rim.

The ride from Flagstaff or Williams to the Grand Canyon is very beautiful. Watch for hawks, antelope, deer, coyote roadrunners, and other wildlife. If you've never seen the canyon before, please follow this procedure. It sounds strange but it's worth the effort.

Enter the park and drive directly to the El Tovar Hotel. Ride up the short hill and park in the lot to the right. Turn and walk directly toward the El Tovar. As you come to the traffic circle in front of the hotel walk to the right toward the rim of the canyon, **but keep your eyes locked on the front of the hotel.** As you reach the wall at the edge of the canyon, turn and look at the Grand Canyon for the first time. I guarantee it will take your breath away.

Be sure to take a walk through the lobby of the El Tovar. It is an exceptionally beautiful hotel. The dining room is very nice and lunch at the El Tovar can be an experience you will never forget. It will also do serious damage to your wallet. The El Tovar is a five star establishment and is worthy of every star. There are a few less expensive places nearby.

In the fall, winter, and spring, private vehicles are allowed to ride the edge of the canyon all the way to Hermit's Rest. In the summer the crowds preclude this adventure and you have to ride shuttle busses. The best way to see the canyon is to ride all the way out to Hermit's Rest, have a cool drink and then ride part way back stopping at about every other overlook. You can't go wrong in your choices and believe it or not, every view is different.

No matter what time of the year you visit the canyon, be sure you don't miss riding the 26 mile scenic ride along Route 64 on the Southern Rim. Stop at the first or second overlook you come to. These are the two only places you can get a "me and my bike at the Grand Canyon" picture. Ride the rest of the 26 miles and stop at the Grand View overlook. It has a massive stone watch tower built in the early 1900's by the Fred Harvey Company to roughly recreate an ancient tower located near Four Corners. It's neat.

North - Grand Canyon. The IMAX Movie.

Please consider stopping in Tusayan (just south of the Grand Canyon) and see the IMAX theater Grand Canyon movie on their 60 foot tall screen! You will see more of, and get a better feel for the Grand Canyon than you did in all the sightseeing you may do during the day. The movie is magnificent. I consider it a "must see," and I'll bet you'll agree, no matter how much they paid the actors, it wasn't enough!

North - Holbrook. The Petrified Forest.

The Petrified Forest is a "ride through" park. You enter at one end and ride through to the other end. The park is 26 miles long and has 20 scenic views. There are two Visitor Centers, one at each end of the Park, and both are worth seeing.

North - Jerome. A Living Ghost Town.

Jerome is a living ghost town perched high on the side of Cleopatra Hill. The first official mining claims in the area were filed in 1876, and the last mine shut down in 1953. At one time 15,000 people lived here. Now it's just a few hundred. The Gold King "gold mine" is down a short dirt road at the hairpin turn in the middle of town. It features a lot of old steam engines and mechanical stuff. It's a tourist trap, but a real neat one. There is also a great museum down the hill in the large white building. It has a model of the several hundred miles of mine shafts below Jerome. If you are hungry the English Kitchen is the oldest restaurant in Arizona and has pretty good food.

North - Meteor Crater.

Called "This Planet's Most Penetrating Natural Attraction", the Meteor Crater is located 35 miles East of Flagstaff on Interstate 40. The crater itself is over a mile across and 570 feet deep, and if that doesn't strike you as big, consider it can hold 20 football fields on the floor of the crater alone.

The crater was formed 49,000,000 years ago when the earth was struck by a huge meteor. The landscape is so moon-like the Apollo Astronauts trained there before their lunar missions.

North - Monument Valley.

You've already seen Monument Valley. I'd say at least a hundred times in car commercials. Now see it for real. Located in the middle of nowhere, Monument Valley straddles the border between Kayenta, Arizona and Mexican Hat, Utah. The road through Monument Valley is paved and easily ridden, and the valley itself is spectacular beyond words. Towering spires of solid rock soar hundreds of feet into the air, carved by wind, sand, and time. Huge rocks, weighing thousands of pounds, seem so delicately balanced that they should fall over in the most gentle wind, and yet have survived millions of years while waiting for you to come by.

I sincerely suggest you stay on the paved roads. If you want to get closer to the scenery, the best way is to stop at Gouldings Trading Post and take one of their Jeep Tours. Even though the dirt roads are smooth and well maintained, the Jeeps will take you places you just cannot go safely on two (touring) wheels.

North - Payson.

Payson is 85 miles northeast of Phoenix on Route 87. Route 87 is a very nice rural highway, and is pleasant to ride. Truthfully, there's not much to do or see in Payson. Not much good food either. It is a good stopping point for gas on your way to Show Low or Strawberry.

North - Prescott. Whiskey Row.

Prescott was the first Arizona State Capitol. Stop at the large old Yavapai County Courthouse. There are parking spaces allocated to bikes only, but be careful as some have deep water drains at the corners. Take a few minutes to rest. There are several restaurants in the area. Whiskey Row is across the street and those are REAL cowboy bars.

North - Prescott. Sharlot Hall Museum.

The Sharlot Hall Museum is just up the street to the west of the courthouse. The original "Governor's Mansion" is there along with one of the best collections of early Arizona artifacts in the state. The museum is named after Sharlot Hall, a true Arizona pioneer, and a heck of a neat lady!

North - Strawberry. Tonto Natural Bridge.

At 183 feet high, 150 feet wide, and 400 feet long, this is the largest travertine bridge in the world and is well worth seeing. However, first a word of caution. Currently the road down to the bridge is 3 miles of hard packed dirt. It's well maintained, but you should stop at the top of the road and check it out on foot before you ride down, as once you start there is no way to turn back. Be especially careful at the very bottom. I watched a GoldWing go down right at the entrance gate. It's not a level as it looks! If the road has been recently graded and is hard packed you can ride it if you are careful. Go lightly on the front brake! If it is loose dirt, sand or gravel, or if you are not comfortable on dirt and gravel, don't do it. The bridge is nice, but it's not worth dying for. The good news is the road is scheduled to be paved in late 1994. Hopefully by the time you read this the paving will be complete.

North - Strawberry. Oldest School in Arizona.

After seeing the Natural Bridge, continue up Route 87 about 3 miles and visit Strawberry.   The food at the Strawberry Lodge is very good, especially the homemade pies. Turn left at the Strawberry Lodge and visit the old Strawberry School.   It's just a few miles down the road, is the oldest schoolhouse in Arizona, and is beautifully restored.   The road beyond the school turns to dirt and is not worth riding. Leave the school and return to Strawberry. In Strawberry turn left and ride 16 miles north to an asphalt road which takes you left (west) to Camp Verde. This is a GREAT RIDING ROAD! It must have been designed for motorcyclists.

North - Williams. Steam Train.

The first steam train service from Williams to the Grand Canyon began in 1901.   Up to that time the journey was by horse or wagon over rough dirt roads.

The train ran up until 1969 when it became unprofitable.   A resurgence of interest in steam trains in the 1980's brought about a complete refurbishing of the tracks and the purchase of "new" old rolling stock. Now the trains run every day in the summer months, and twice a week in the winter. Call 1-800-THE-TRAIN for more information.

North - Wickenburg. Vulture Mine.

Wickenburg is just 62 miles northwest of Phoenix. Leave Phoenix by riding 20 miles north on Interstate 17, The Black Canyon Freeway, to Route 74. Turn left and head west 42 miles to Wickenburg. There is an interesting scenic overlook on the way at Lake Pleasant if you'd like to see the new dam and the lake itself. Stop for breakfast in Wickenburg at the Gold Nugget restaurant. There's easy parking in the back.

The Vulture Mine was started by Henry Wickenburg. The story is he bent over to pick up a vulture he had shot and saw the ground was laced with gold. The Vulture Mine is closed now, but the old buildings and machinery are still standing. It's privately owned and admission is inexpensive. The walking tour of the area is self guided and can be hot in the summer months. Be sure to bring a hat and carry water.

The Vulture Mine is located about 10 miles west of Wickenburg on Route 60. Watch for Vulture Mine Road. Turn south and follow the road to the mine. The parking lot and last 100 yards of the access road are not paved, so be careful.

North - Yarnell. Yarnell Hill and Frog Rock.

Yarnell Hill is just 22 miles Northwest of Wickenburg. Leave Wickenburg by turning right onto Rt. 93 and then bearing right onto Route 89. After you go through Congress and cross over a (dry) river bridge (1.2 miles) watch the west skyline for our famous "Frog Rock". It's very green. Continue on to Yarnell Hill, but please be very careful. It's a two lane divided road up the side of a mountain and the curves get tighter at the top. There are several opportunities to run off the road, and off the side of the mountain.

North - Yarnell. Shrine of St. Joseph.

The Catholic Shrine of Saint Joseph is in Yarnell. It is the Stations of the Cross with full size figures of Christ. It is built into the side of a mountain and is very restful and serene.

Eastern Arizona Attractions.

East - Show Low. The Mogollon Rim.

Show Low is an interesting town located northeast of Phoenix on the Mogollon Rim (Mogy-yon Rim). Show Low was named after a card game in which two ranchers, Corydon Cooley and Marion Clark, settled their differences. Rather than drawing guns, they agreed to each draw a card, with the low card to be the winner and the loser to leave town. Cooley drew a deuce. Nobody remembers what Clark drew.

The Mogollon Rim cuts east/west across 300 miles of Arizona and forms a natural separation between the low and high country. Stop and enjoy the beauty as you look down 300 to 2000 foot tall sheer cliffs. This beautiful area is the country Zane Grey wrote about in his novels. His hunting cabin was near here but was destroyed by "The Dude" forest fire in 1990. Enjoy the ride on Route 260 as it is one of Arizona's most beautiful roads. You'll pass through Overgaard and Heber and come to Show Low. The ride from Payson is about 83 miles.

East - Show Low. The Salt River Canyon.

Just south of Show Low is one of the most spectacular riding attractions in Arizona, the Salt River Canyon. The canyon is 2000 feet deep and you ride into and back out of it in less than 10 miles. Stop at the bottom and have a cool drink at the little general store. The "Salt River Jail" next to the store is interesting in its own right.

East - Eagar. The Little House Museum.

A unique museum nestled in the canyon walls of the Little Colorado River featuring a well presented collection of historical photos and antiques that illustrate the life and times of the original settlers. Ride seven miles East of Eagar on Rt. 260 and turn south on South Fork Road. Ride three miles (all paved except for the last half mile) to the museum. Open May through September. 602-333-2286

East - The Coronado Trail.

The Coronado Trail Scenic Byway follows the route Coronado traveled as he searched for the "Seven Cities of Cibola" over 450 years ago. This byway was the first highway built with federal aid money. It used to be numbered Rt. 666 and was called "The Devil's Highway". It's been renumbered Rt. 191 but believe me, it is still a "Devil of a Highway". The ride from Springerville/Eagar to Morenci can best be described as "intense". It's not relaxing, but is some of the finest riding in America. The road is smooth, twisty, beautiful, well maintained, and a joy to behold. But it does take effort to ride it.

Watch for the "pin-cushion tree" at about 9 miles south of the Blue Vista overlook. It's a tall dead tree on the edge of the road that bow hunters have taken to shooting full of hunting arrows. There are hundreds of rainbow colored arrows sticking out of that old tree!

For a bit of local history stop at the overlook at about the 176.5 mile mark. Look up the hill and you'll see a grave site inside a fenced area. This is the grave of Charles Allen Hamblin. Mr. Hamblin was the son of Lyman Stoddard Hamblin, and Esther Cecelia (Burk) Hamblin. Lyman Hamblin was a carpenter and fiddler, Esther was a mid-wife. The Hamblins came to Arizona from Utah at the direction of the Mormon Church (LDS). The church's purpose was to populate the remote parts of the Southwest and to spread the word of the church. The Hamblins had ten children, 7 boys and 3 girls. The last five were born in the Springerville/Eagar area. Charles was born in Farmington, Utah.

Charles Hamblin was cutting timber in the area for use as mining props. He came down with smallpox and died on February 10th, 1899. His partner buried him there on the side of the hill. In those days news traveled slowly and it was quite a while before word of his death reached his parents. Eventually the family arranged for a headstone and Lyman and Esther and several brothers and sisters came to put it in place in about 1939. Visit the grave and say hello to Mr. Hamblin if you wish, but please treat the site with respect. He was there before you arrived, and he'll be there after you leave. It's his home you're visiting.

My thanks to Marion and Burma Hamblin of Eagar, AZ for this information.

Southern Arizona Attractions.

South - Bisbee.

In the early 1900's Bisbee was the largest town in Arizona. People came from all over the world to visit, and the accommodations were as fine as in any European capital.

Bisbee is named after Judge DeWitt Bisbee of San Francisco, California. The judge was responsible for arranging the financing which made mining in the local area profitable. Although the town is named after him, the judge never visited Bisbee.

An interesting story centers on the individual who originally found the ore that made Bisbee famous. The fellow was George Warren and he lost ownership of his mining claim when he bet another man he could outrun a horse on a 100 yard course. The bet wasn't as foolish as it sounds. It can be done, but not if you're drunk. Warren was, the horse wasn't. He lost what eventually became one of the richest mining claims in the world.

Be sure to visit "Brewery Gulch" in downtown Bisbee. The "Gulch" was named after the original brewery owned by Mr. A. B. Seiber in 1881. At one time there were over 47 saloons on the street, and they were frequented by cowboys, ranchers, businessmen, and "professional ladies". "Big Nose Katie Elder", "Doc" Holiday's girlfriend, is said to have practiced her profession in "Brewery Gulch" before moving up to Tombstone.

South - Bisbee. The Lavender Pit and Queen Mines.

Twenty-one beautiful miles southeast of Tombstone is Bisbee, home of the Lavender Pit and Copper Queen Mines. The Lavender Pit mine is in the center of town and is huge. Today it stands idle, waiting for copper prices to rise and make it worthwhile to work it again.

Farther down the main road, just as it curves around to the west, is the Queen Mine. This is a more traditional underground mine and is open to the public. The tour is on electric trains and the guides are miners who used to work in the mine. It is a very interesting trip into another world.

For good food, try The Copper Queen Hotel. It has a great restaurant.

South - Coolidge. Casa Grande National Monument.

Always remember, and never forget, the Casa Grande ruins are not in Casa Grande, they are in Coolidge.   And Coolidge is just 9 miles southwest of Florence on Route 287-West.

The Casa Grande (Big House) ruins are huge, containing 11 rooms in a multi-story structure.   Built by the Hohokam Indians, Casa Grande dates back to the 1300's.   There are indications the structure served as a type of calendar as some of the windows line up with the sun on Summer Solstice.   The ruins are well preserved, well presented, and very accessible.

South - Dragoon. The Amerind Foundation.

The Amerind (AMERican INDian) Foundation is located in Dragoon, Arizona, 64 miles east of Tucson, and just one mile south of Interstate 10 at Exit 318. It is just past Benson on the way to Willcox. The foundation was created in 1937 by William Shirley Fulton, an archeologist and collector of American Indian artifacts.   His life's collection of ethnographic and archeological materials is on display and fills both floors of a huge Spanish style hacienda.   A second building houses a fascinating and extensive collection of Western Art. The telephone number is 602-586-3666.

South - Oracle Junction. Biosphere II.

Oracle Junction is 102 miles southeast of Phoenix, and 28 miles Northeast of Tucson.   Its current claim to fame is the Biosphere II scientific experiment. Biosphere II (the Earth is Biosphere I) is a huge, glass, self contained, self sufficient structure which replicates all of the earth's major environments, from desert to rain forest. Several scientists lived in the closed structure for two years to study the environment under controlled conditions.   There is a tour available, a gift shop, a hotel, and other services.

South - Globe/Miami. Copper Country

Globe is easily reached from Phoenix or Show Low. This is copper country
and Globe was a mining town. The copper boom is over for the time being
and the town is in depression. It will be interesting to see it come back if
copper prices rise as there is plenty of ore still in the mines.

Just west of Globe is Miami. The ore from the surrounding mines was
brought to Miami for reduction and smelting. The huge mountains of grey
and tan dirt along the roadway are the "tailings" from the smelting process.
They've been there for decades and are almost totally devoid of nutrients.
The towns have started laying straw on the hills and planting grass. The plan
is to herd cattle on the slopes and make the replanting pay for itself. I hope
it works because the tailings are an embarrassment as they are now.

South - Florence. Prison Museum & McFarland State Park.

Florence is located 60 miles southeast of Phoenix. As you approach from
the north look to the right and you'll see a hill in the distance with a
pyramid on top. That's the tomb of Charles Debrille Poston, the "Father
of Arizona". Poston was responsible for getting Arizona admitted to
Statehood.

Florence is a quiet little town and is very representative of rural Arizona
living. The primary industry here is the Florence State Prison. You'll see
it to the east as you ride into the area. Turn into Florence and ride to the
main street. McFarland State Park is to the north end of town, the Pinal
County Historical Museum is at the south end. Both are well worth
seeing. The Pinal Museum has quite a few artifacts from the prison,
including a bizarre collection of (used) hanging nooses.

While in town, notice the tower on the Court House. The hands on the
clock are painted on! The town ran out of funds when they built the
Court House and never did put in a clock movement. It's become so well
known they can't change it.

South - Florence. The Tom Mix Monument.

Just 17 miles south of Florence on Route 79 is the Tom Mix Monument.
The cowboy movie star was killed here in 1940 when he drove his 1937
Cord convertible off the road. The monument shows his horse "Tony"
standing riderless.

South - Tubac. Mission Tumacacori Ruins.

The communities of Tubac/Tumacacori exemplify the term "quaint". These towns were thriving long before George Washington began irritating the British Red Coats. The mission ruins are magnificent and date back to 1600's, having been established under the direction of the Jesuit priest, Father Eusebio Francisco Kino. The mission was rebuilt in its current form in the 1800's by the Franciscan Order. The mission ruins, schoolhouse, museum, and shops are all open to the public. It's well worth seeing.

South - Tucson.

Tucson was founded in 1775, but had been visited by the Spanish missionary, Father Eusebio Francisco Kino as early as 1687. At that time the area was inhabited by the Pima Indians and named "Stjukshon". The Pima's settlement had previously been inhabited by the Hohokam Indians, known as the "vanished ones."

Tucson is also known as "The Old Pueblo", and when you think of Tucson you naturally think of the Old West. This is very accurate as Tucson is the oldest continually inhabited settlement in America! However, Tucson is also a thoroughly modern city, and is one of only 14 cities in America with a complete complement of the performing arts, with ballet, symphony, theater, and opera companies.

South - Tucson. Mission San Xavier del Bac.

Also known as "The White Dove of the Desert", this mission is the oldest in Arizona. Father Eusebio Francisco Kino founded the settlement in 1700 at a location the Papago Indians called "Bac", which means "where the waters gathered." The mission was started in 1778 and is built of fired brick on a foundation of volcanic rock. It is currently undergoing restoration but is open to the public. An interesting legend says the right hand bell tower was left uncapped as a tribute to a young priest who fell from it to his death during construction.

South - Tucson. Old Tucson Movie Town.

Arizona is a natural setting for making western movies. Hollywood discovered this back in 1939 and built Old Tucson for the movie "Arizona". Since then over 200 movies have been made there.   Now known as "Hollywood in the Desert", it's still being used today, and having a moving picture in production while you're visiting is not uncommon. I've had it happen twice. Old Tucson is a complete recreation of the Tucson of the 1860's. One interesting tidbit is the doorways on one side of Main Street are smaller than the doorways on the other side. This allows shorter actors to appear to be taller as they enter the buildings.

South - Tucson. Titan Missile Silo.

This is real. It's not a mock up, not a training silo, not a dummy. This was an actual Titan Missile Silo that helped keep the peace for a lot of years. The missile in the silo is so complete the U.S. Government had to agree to have a transparent cover on the silo and a plexiglass window in the missile's nose cone so Russian satellites could monitor it and ensure it could never be made operational. The control center, living quarters, silo, and all support areas are included in the tour.

South - Tucson. Sonoran Desert Museum.

Don't be misled by the name. This museum is actually one of the world's finest zoological parks.   The presentation of the animals is first class. Every animal is in a natural, no bars environment and it's incredible to stand eye to eye with mountain lions, tigers, big horn sheep, and other desert dwellers. In my book (and this is my book) this is a "must see". I kid you not.

South - Tucson. Pima Air Museum.

Do you like airplanes? This museum, because of its proximity to Davis-Monthan AFB has one of just about everything! They have over 200 aircraft on display, ranging from the dawn of aviation to the most modern times, and you get to get real up close and personal. Consider walking around touching B47, B52, B57, B58 Bombers, F100, F101, F102, F104, F105, F107 (one of only two built) fighters, X-1, X-15, and other X-Planes.   They even have a SR-71 Blackbird on display. If you love airplanes as I do, allow a full day for this museum. It's fantastic.

South - Tucson. Saguaro National Monument.

This National Monument consists of two totally separate areas. The East Monument (Park) is east of I-10, the West Monument (Park) is west of I-10. Both are spectacular.

The western monument is 5 miles west of I-10 on Route 86. The turn off is a small road going north. The park is about 12 miles down the road, past Old Tucson and the Sonoran Desert Museum. It's very pretty, very relaxing, and has a nice visitor's center. The road is graded dirt, but is kept in good condition.

The eastern monument is best accessed by taking exit 281 off I-10. Ride through the small town of Vail and continue 14 miles to the monument. The road is paved, and makes a 10 mile loop through the end of the park.

South - Tucson. Mt. Lemmon.

The hardest part of this lovely day ride is finding your way across Tucson to the Catalina Highway, the road to Mt. Lemmon. One way is to cruise up or down Interstate 10 until you find the Speedway Boulevard exit. Once on Speedway, ride East to Houghton Road. Turn left onto Houghton Road (North) and it will take you to the Catalina Highway. Turn right (East) onto the Catalina Highway.

Mount Lemmon has the distinction of being the only mountain in the U.S. named after the first woman to climb it. The ride is 35 miles of easy riding, beautiful scenery. There are several interesting places to stop as you ride up the mountain, including the ruins of an old prison. The ski area at the top of the mountain has a nice restaurant. There are also telescopes on the mountain but the area is closed to visitors.

Once at the top the only way down is to ride back the way you came. The road actually continues up and over the mountain, but becomes dirt and gravel and suited only for four wheel drive vehicles. Don't even think about riding it.

Come on back down the mountain and pick up Houghton Road going south. Watch for signs to the Saguaro National Monument. It's only about a 10 mile ride. The loop through the monument is another 10 miles, but a prettier 10 miles you'll be hard pressed to find. When you leave the monument, turn South toward Vail and pick up Interstate 10 at exit 271. From here it's a fast 20 miles back to Tucson.

South - Tucson. Kitt Peak Observatories.

This is a great day ride if you're in the mood for some laid back, easy riding. Sleep late in the morning and head west on Route 86 about 10AM. Ride due west for about 40 miles to Route 386, the Kitt Peak turn off. There's no sense in leaving earlier as the road is closed prior to 10AM.

The 12 mile ride up to the 6900 foot summit is spectacular. It's full of twisty-turnies and is a favorite road for the cafe' racer set. Be careful though, there are plenty of decreasing radius turns and it's real easy to get in over your head. The drop offs over the edge of the road are spectacular also, so try not to try one!

Kitt Peak has been used as a site for telescopes since 1958. It has 20 telescopes on it now and they operate around the clock all year long. Most are owned by universities, a few by governments. One of the most spectacular is the solar telescope as it is over 500 feet long. Two hundred feet of the telescope is above ground, the other three hundred feet is below ground.

Kitt Peak has a nice visitor's center with free videos, tours of some of the observatories, and a picnic area. There are no food facilities, so bring your own snacks. Hours are 10AM to 4PM. The phone number is 620-5350.

South - Tucson. Davis-Monthan Air Force Base.

The term "bone-yard" is not appreciated by the men and women who serve on this Air Force storage and salvage base. This is where the Air Force stores surplus aircraft and eventually recycles the individual parts. Examples of the most historic planes are lined up on Celebrity Row and tours are available. Call them at 602-750-3204.

South - Tucson. Tombstone.

Tombstone is southeast of Tucson by 70 miles and 100 years. Tombstone is not a movie prop town. This is real. This is where such famous and infamous characters as Wyatt and Virgil Earp, Doc Holiday, Bat Masterson, and Johnny Ringo walked, talked, and killed. Visit the OK Corral. Stand where the Earps and Doc Holiday stood when they faced the Clanton Brothers. Then visit Boot Hill and say hello to the Clanton brothers. They're still there.

Consider visiting the Rose Tree Inn Museum. The museum part is fascinating and the Rose Tree itself covers over 7,000 square feet. It was planted in 1885 and is listed in the Guinness Book of Records as the largest single rose bush in the world.

There are over 50 interesting things to do or see in Tombstone. Drop by the Chamber of Commerce office on Allen Street and grab a "Guide to Tombstone" brochure. They're nice folks and very helpful.

South - Willcox. Apple Pie.

If you're in Willcox and hungry for some great apple pie, cross over to the north side of I-10, and turn right onto Circle I Road. Then look for Stout's Cider Mill. They've got just about the best pie I've ever eaten. There's an Arizona Tourist Information Center there also.

South - Willcox. Dos Cabezas.

Ride south of Willcox on Route 186 about 19 miles and consider stopping at the "ghost town" of Dos Cabezas. There's not much of the town left, but the cemetery is very interesting, and the headstones are very poignant.

Dos Cabezas is Spanish for "Two Heads", so look for two bald summits nearby. The town was founded in 1857 as a stage stop on the Birch Route (although the sign on the old stage stop says "Butterfield Stage"). Prior to that it had been used as a stop on the pony express run from El Paso to Tucson. Silver and gold mines provided the life blood of the town, but weren't enough to keep it going through the draught of 1911. The town died but about 30 hardy souls still live there.

South - Willcox. Chiricahua National Monument.

The Chiricahua National Monument is 32 miles southeast of Willcox on Route 186. Stop at the entrance and visit the family grave of the Ericsons. These Swedish immigrants operated the Faraway Ranch near the current park. The ranch was later converted to a guest ranch. The ranch is accessible by walking a quarter mile trail off to the left, just as you enter the park. Because of the interest the Ericsons sparked in the beautiful surroundings the area was declared a National Park in 1924.

The Ericsons loved the area and the inscription on one of the plaques speaks of their feelings. "They carved a home from the wilderness with the warp of labor and the woof of dreams. They wove a pattern of life as beautiful as the sunsets and as enduring as the mountains they loved so well."

The Chiricahua Mountains are the home of the Chiricahua Apache Indians, the most famous was Geronimo. He used these canyons, culverts, and caves for ten years to hide from the soldiers from Fort Bowie who were searching for him under the command of General George Crook. He was finally captured in 1866 because General Crook employed other Apaches as scouts and they led him to Geronimo. Geronimo was eventually imprisoned at Fort Sill, Oklahoma. He died there and is buried in a special cemetery dedicated to the Indians imprisoned there. The cemetery there is peaceful and well maintained, (I've visited it) and Geronimo's grave is quite dignified, but his people really want him returned to Arizona.

The visitor's center is a two mile ride from the entrance and is worth seeing. The ride to Massai Point is about 10 miles and the point is 6900 feet high. The views are spectacular.

South - Willcox. Cochise's Stronghold.

When you leave the Chiricahua National Monument, turn left (South) onto Route 181. Follow it 23 miles to where it connects with Route 191. Turn right (North). About 7 miles up the road is the turn off (left) to Cochise's Stronghold. It was from here this Apache warrior rode roughshod over the earlier settlers in the area. Cochise died here in 1874 and it is said his braves buried him and rode their ponies over his grave to obliterate all signs of the site. Access to the stronghold is 10 miles of rough dirt road followed by a 3 mile hike. Unless you are on a dual sport bike I'd suggest you pass on by.

Continue past the stronghold turn off and ride another 7 miles to the turn off (left) to Dragoon. This is a small, paved road and it will take you back to Interstate 10 at mile marker 318. Once you hit I-10, you've got a 67 mile ride back to Tucson. It should take about 90 minutes.

South - Willcox. Cowboy Museums.

The Cowboy Hall of Fame Museum is housed in the Chamber of Commerce Visitor Center in Willcox, Arizona. It has an interesting collection of artifacts from local ranches and Indians.

The Rex Allen Arizona Cowboy Museum is located on Rail Road Avenue. It houses an extensive collection of memorabilia from the career of the famous cowboy movie star Rex Allen. Telephone: 602-384-2272 for both of these museums.

Western Arizona Attractions.

West - Lake Havasu. London Bridge.

The story goes that the purchasers of the London Bridge thought they were buying London's "Tower Bridge", a beautiful, twin towered drawbridge. The crafty sellers are said to have allowed this misconception to continue until the sale was so far along it couldn't be stopped. Then they showed the buyers the much less grand London Bridge they had purchased.

This all happened in 1967. It seemed the founders of Lake Havasu City were looking for something to make their three year old city stand out from the rest of Arizona's offerings. At about the same time the London Bridge, after having served well since 1830, was declared to be in need of too much repair to be worth keeping. The city fathers put it up for sale.

Lake Havasu City paid $2,500,000 for the bridge and had it disassembled and shipped to California. From there it was trucked to Lake Havasu and put back together. The whole process took three years and cost an additional $5,000,000. But it was worth it! Even before the bridge was complete, the word of this audacious project catapulted Lake Havasu City into the national and international headlines and the city began to grow at a phenomenal rate.

Now, I don't believe the story of the bridge's mistaken identity, but it's fun to imagine what would have happened when reality raised its ugly head and the buyers realized they had bought just a rather plain (but big) stone bridge.

The story may not be true, but one thing is certain, the bridge is well worth seeing. In its past it may have been only one of several stone bridges over the River Thames, but in its current setting it's the jewel in the crown of Lake Havasu City.

West - Oatman. A Living Ghost Town.

Oatman is a fun place. Founded in 1851, it's now a Ghost Town, but a very lively one. Oatman is a hold over from the gold rush days when mining paid big time. It dried up the 1930's when the ore played out, but some stubborn, hardy souls stayed behind and the town took on a new persona as a place to go and kick back in an old western setting.

One of the neatest things about Oatman are the burros that come down from the surrounding hills every day and roam the streets looking for handouts from the tourists. These truly are wild animals. They're descended from miner's burros set free when the mines closed. They're so much a part of the town the local stores sell small bags of horse pellets just for feeding the little beggars.

Oatman's current claim to fame is that it is at the end of the last section of Historic Route 66. It used to be a "major" stopping point on the road until Interstate 40 bypassed it. Now it just sleeps in the sun and waits for those hardy souls who want to feed a stray burro.

West - Las Vegas, Nevada.

Las Vegas. Glitter Gulch. The town that never sleeps. The only place where you'll see a little old lady wearing a mink coat, sitting in a Cadillac, counting nickels. It's all that and more.

It's also the Marriage Capital of the World. Instant marriages, 24 hours a day in any one of more than 40 marriage chapels. No waiting, no blood tests, just step right up and say your "I Do's." (Cheryl and I did!) Naturally, the shows are overwhelming, the gambling everywhere, and the casino lights unbelievable.

Now the bad part. The ride to Las Vegas is dangerous. Very dangerous. The main road between Phoenix and Las Vegas is Route 93. This two lane rural highway is known as "Blood Alley" and is the most dangerous strip of road in Arizona. Be careful, and watch for oncoming cars passing in your lane. The little white crosses by the roadside mark fatal accidents. Don't become a white cross.

To me, the best part of going to Las Vegas is Hoover Dam, so stop and take the tour through this huge monolith. The tours run every 30 minutes and are very popular. I figure they make as much money on the tours as they do on the electricity the dam generates. By the way, if you saw the movie, "Universal Soldier", the dam the soldiers liberated was Hoover Dam.

Hoover Dam was completed in 1935. The full story of the construction is told best in a free movie at the visitor's center in Boulder City. It is really interesting! Watch for the signs in town. The visitor's center looks like a very small souvenir store, which it is, but the film is fascinating.

West - Yuma. Territorial Prison.

The Yuma Territorial Prison was built in 1875. Yuma was chosen because of its remoteness from the rest of the state. Escapees, it was reasoned, would have a tough time of it trying to get across the surrounding deserts. The prison was called "The Hell-Hole of Arizona" by its inmates, and a "Country Club" by its detractors. The "Country Club" designation was because it was rather advanced for its time, offering a library, school, and hospital.

The prison housed more than 3,000 men and up to 29 women over its 34 year life. It closed in 1909 and was used briefly as a school when the local high school burned down.

The prison is now open to the public and offers a fascinating view into what was considered to be one of the toughest prisons in America. The museum is full of photographs and memorabilia. The number is 602-783-4771.

West - Yuma. Other Attractions.

While in Yuma check out the Century House Museum. This is one of the oldest structures in Yuma as it was built in 1879. Also see the Peanut Patch for a free tour of the peanut processing facilities. The number is 800-872-7688.

Fort Yuma was built in the 1850's and is one of the earliest forts built in Arizona. There is a nice museum on the Quechan Indians on the fort in an old adobe building. Call 602-572-0661

There is also a camel breeding farm in Yuma. Call 602-627-2553. Last but not least the US Army Quartermaster Depot is well presented by guides dressed in turn of the 1800's costumes. The number is 602-329-0404.

**These saguaros seem to be beckoning to another trail, but we'll stay on
the paved road, thank you!**

(Photo by author)

Campgrounds.

There's plenty of camping available in Arizona. Most of the state is listed as "open camping", meaning you can camp anywhere as long as it's not posted "No Camping", or "Camping in Campgrounds Only". But be careful to not trespass on private land, as sometimes the distinction is not very obvious. For commercial campgrounds try KOA. They're everywhere.

Commercial Camping:

KOA	Kampgrounds of America	800-548-7063

Public Campground Information:

ASP	Arizona State Parks	602-542-4174
NPS	National Parks Service	602-640-5250
USF	US Forest Service	800-283-2267
MAC	Maricopa County Parks	602-262-3711
MOC	Mohave County Parks	602-753-6106
NTP	Navajo Tribal Parks	602-871-6659
PCP	Pima County Parks	602-740-2690

Northwest:

Bonito	NPS	Northwest
Desert View	NPS	Northwest
Grand Canyon - North Rim	NPS	Northwest
Grand Canyon - South Rim	NPS	Northwest
Lees Ferry	NPS	Northwest
Canyon de Chelly	NPS	Northwest
Mitten View	NTP	Northwest
Navajo National Monument	NPS	Northwest
Wahweap	NPS	Northwest

Central/South:

Black Canyon Shooting Range	MAC	Central/South
Lost Dutchman	ASP	Central/South
McDowell Mountain	MAC	Central/South
Usery Mountain	MAC	Central/South
White Tanks	MAC	Central/South
Catalina	ASP	Central/South
Gilbert Ray	PCP	Central/South
Picacho Peak	ASP	Central/South

Central/East:

Big Lake	USF	Central/East
Lyman Lake	ASP	Central/East
Rolf C. Hoyer	USF	Central/East
Canyon Point	USF	Central/East

South:

Organ Pipe Nat'l Monument	NPS	South
Patagonia Lake	ASP	South
Bonita Canyon	NPS	South
Roper Lake	ASP	South

West:

Dead Horse Ranch	ASP	West
Temple Bar	NPS	West
Katherine Landing	NPS	West
Hualapai Mountain	MOC	West
Windsor Beach	ASP	West
Cattail Cove	ASP	West
Buckskin Mountain	ASP	West
Alamo Lake	ASP	West

Hotel and Motel Accommodations.

Arizona offers every type of accommodation from POSH (Port Out Starboard Home, by the way) world class resorts with every possible amenity, to simple Mom and Pop tourist courts and Bed and Breakfasts. There is a list of Bed and Breakfast reservation numbers, and major hotel reservation 800 numbers in the front of this book in the **Important Telephone Numbers** section.

In larger towns, such as Phoenix, Flagstaff, Kingman, Tucson, and others, you'll have plenty of places to choose from. In the smaller towns there are fewer options and you should consider calling ahead to be sure of having a warm room waiting. This is especially true if it is "in season", April to September. However, in all the years I've been touring Arizona I have NEVER, EVER, not been able to find a place to stay, no matter how much "in season" it was, or how crowded the town. On the other hand I have also slept in some pretty sleazy motels now and then because of not calling ahead.

Be sure to try some of our Bed and Breakfasts. Even though I like luxury hotels, I like B&B's even better. I find it very enjoyable to have a host I can meet and have a friendly chat with at the end of the day. So, if you want to try some real western hospitality stay at a few B&B's. Call the B&B services and ask for a directory. They can also make reservations for you anywhere in the state. Buy the way, you can often get into a B&B when all the motel rooms in town are booked up.

The following are some of the hotels, motels, and B&B's I've stayed in, or had recommended by friends or clients. I don't include any pricing indicators because the prices vary quite a bit depending on the size of the facility, the number of rooms, the level of luxury, the season of the year, the proprietor's mood, and your attitude.

Alpine, AZ.
Tal-wi-wi Lodge   602-339-4319

Bisbee, AZ.
Bisbee Inn B&B   602-432-5131
Bisbee Grand Hotel B&B   602-432-5900
Copper Queen Hotel   602-432-2216
Clawson House B&B   602-432-5237
El Rancho Motel   602-432-2293
The White House B&B   602-432-7215

Boulder, NV.
Motel 8   702-294-8888

Cameron, AZ.
Cameron Trading Post   602-679-2231

Canyon de Chelly (Chinle, AZ).
Canyon de Chelly Motel   602-674-5875
Thunderbird Lodge   602-674-5841
Holiday Inn   602-674-5000
Navajo Nation Lodge   602-871-4108
 (Window Rock, AZ)

Clifton, AZ.
The Potter Ranch B&B   602-865-4847

Cortez, CO.
Bel Rau Motel   303-565-3738
The Cortez Inn   303-565-6000
Sands Best Western   303-565-3761
Turquoise Motor Inn   303-565-3778

Cottonwood, AZ.
Cottonwood Inn (Best Western)   602-634-5575
View Motel   602-634-7581
Flying Eagle B&B   602-634-0211

Death Valley, CA.
Stove Pipe Wells   619-786-2387
Furnace Creek Inn   619-786-2302
Stagecoach Casino   702-553-2419

Durango, CO.
Red Lion Inn 303-547-8010
Rio Grande Inn 303-385-4980

Eagar/Springerville, AZ.
Paisley Corner B&B 602-333-4665

Flagstaff, AZ.
Little America 602-779-7918
Travelodge 800-255-3050
Quality Inn 800-228-5151
Best Westerns 800-524-1234
Dierker House B&B 602-774-3249
Birch Tree Inn B&B 602-774-1042

Globe, AZ.
Cloud Nine Motel 800-432-6655
Nostsger Hill Inn B&B 602-425-2260

Grand Canyon - South Rim.
National Park Lodges 602-638-2401
Tusayan Best Western 602-638-2681
Quality Inn 602-638-2673

Grand Canyon - North Rim.
TWA Services 801-586-7686
Kaibab Lodge 602-638-2389
Jacob Lake 602-643-7232

Jerome, AZ.
The Connor Hotel. 602-634-5792
The Cottage Inn 602-634-0701
The Miner's Roost 602-634-5094
Nancy Russel's B&B 602-634-3270
Sulivan House B&B 602-634-2200

Kayenta, AZ.
Anasazi Inn 602-697-3793
Holiday Inn 602-674-5687
Wetherill Inn 602-697-3231
Canyon Inn at Tsegi 602-697-3793
Courtyards by Marriott 800-234-6835

Keams Canyon, AZ.
Keams Canyon Motel   602-738-2297

Kingman, AZ.
Days Inn   800-446-6900
Rodeway Inn   800-228-2000
Quality Inn   800-221-2222

Lake Havasu, AZ.
Nautical Inn   602-855-2141
Travelodge   602-680-9202
EZ-8 Motel   602-855-4023

Lakeside, AZ.
Lakeview Lodge & Cabins   602-368-5253
Econo-Lodge   602-367-3636
The Coldstream B&B   602-369-0115
Whispering Pines Resort   602-367-4386

Las Vegas, NV.
Four Queens Casino   800-634-6045
California Casino   800-634-6255
Motel 8 (Boulder, NV)   702-294-8888

Mexican Hat, UT.
Canyonlands Motel   801-683-2230
Mexican Hat Lodge   801-683-2222
San Juan Inn   800-447-2022

Monument Valley, UT.
Gouldings' Lodge   801-727-3231
See also: Kayenta
See also: Mexican Hat

Page, AZ.
Courtyards by Marriott   800-234-6835

Payson, AZ.
Majestic Mountain Inn   602-474-0185

Phoenix, AZ

Biltmore	602-954-2579
Courtyards by Marriott	602-944-7373
Crescent Hotel	602-943-8200
Hampton Inn	602-864-6233
Motel 6	602-995-7592
Travel Lodge	602-995-9500
Premier Inns	602-943-2371
Wyndham Hotel	602-220-4400

Pinetop, AZ.
See "Lakeside"

Prescott, AZ.

The Hassayampa Inn	602-778-9434
The Vendome Hotel	602-776-0900
Country Inn B&B	602-445-7991
Mt. Vernon Inn B&B	800-574-7284
Prescott Pines Inn B&B	800-541-5374
The Senator Inn B&B	602-445-1440

Sedona, AZ.

Sky Ranch Lodge	602-282-6400
Lantern Light Inn B&B	602-282-3419
Oak Creek Terrace	602-282-3562
Slide Rock Lodge	602-282-3531
Quality Inn	602-282-7151
Matterhorn Inn	602-282-7176
Arroyo Roble	602-282-4001
Don Hoel's Cabins	800-292-4635
Outpost (Referral Service)	602-282-5112
Kennedy House B&B	602-282-1624

Show Low, AZ.

K C Motel	602-537-4422
Paint Pony Lodge	602-537-5773
Apache Pines Motel	602-537-4542
Thunderbird Motel	602-537-4391
Kiva Motel	602-537-4542
Whiting Inn	602-537-7694

Springerville/Eagar, AZ.
Paisley Corner B&B   602-333-4665

Strawberry, AZ.
Strawberry Lodge   602-476-3333
Windmill Corner Inn   602-476-3064
Strawberry Hill Cabins   602-476-4252

Teec Nos Pos, AZ.
Navaho Tribal Hotel   602-674-3618

Tombstone, AZ.
Adobe Lodge   602-457-2223
Hacienda Huachuca Motel   602-457-2201
Larian Motel   602-457-2272
Lookout Lodge   602-457-2223
Tombstone Boarding House (B&B)   602-457-3716
Tombstone Motel   602-457-3478
Buford House B&B   602-457-3168
Pricilla's B&B   602-457-3844

Torrey, UT.
Rim Rock Motel   801-425-3843
Capitol Reef Inn   801-425-3271

Tuba City, AZ.
Tuba City Motel   602-283-4545

Tubac/Tumacacori, AZ.
The Old Mission B&B   602-398-9583
Rancho Santa Cruz   602-281-8383
Rio Rico Resort   602-281-1910

Tucson, AZ.
Arizona Inn (very historic)   602-325-1541
Best Western (on Drachman)   602-791-7551
Embassy Suites   602-745-2700
Sheraton El Conquistador   602-742-7000
The Lodge on the Desert   800-456-5634

Willcox, AZ.

Best Western Plaza Inn	602-384-3556
Cochise Hotel	602-384-3156
Comfort Inn	602-384-4222
Desert Breeze Motel	602-384-4636
Motel 6	602-384-2201
Royal Western Lodge	602-384-2266
Triangle T Guest Ranch	602-586-7533
(Dragoon, AZ)	
Kelly's Whistlestop B&B	602-586-7515
(Dragoon, AZ)	

Williams, AZ.

Canyon Country Inn B&B	800-456-0682
The Johnstonian B&B	602-635-2178
Stagecoach Motel	602-637-2278
Copper State Motel	602-637-2335

Window Rock, AZ.

Navaho Nation Inn	602-871-4108

Yuma, AZ.

Travelodge	800-255-3050
Holiday Inn	800-465-4329
Casa De Osgood B&B	602-342-0471
Lazy A Ranch B&B	602-627-2827

Montezuma's Castle near Camp Verde, AZ
(Photo courtesy Arizona Office of Tourism)

About the Author.

Frank Del Monte bought his first motorcycle when he was 15 years old. The bike was a two-stroke, 125cc Harley-Davidson "Tele-Glide", and he immediately rode it 75 miles to visit his sister and her new husband. He's been hooked on motorcycle touring ever since.

In 1975 he founded the United States Norton Owners Association. Since then, this club, now named "The International Norton Owners Association" has grown to over 8000 members, all dedicated to the preservation and enjoyment of the famed British marque.

Frank considers himself to be a native of Arizona who, through an accident of birth, was born in Washington DC. Frank moved to Phoenix, Arizona in 1978 and in 1988 started Western States Motorcycle Tours, Inc. This company rents touring motorcycles for use in the Southwest. This book is the result of his clients asking, "Where should I go? What should I see?"

Frank's next book is in the works and will be on touring Colorado.

* * *

Author on Historic Rt. 66

CACTUS COUNTRY

Before you touch, read this fascinating book on cactus of the Southwest deserts. The many illustrations and humorous cartoons make this trip through the desert one to remember! By Jim and Sue Willoughby.

5 1/2 x 8 1/2—112 pages . . . $6.95

SNAKES and other REPTILES of the SOUTHWEST

This book is a must for hikers, hunters, campers and all outdoor enthusiasts! More than 80 photographs and illustrations in the text and a full color plate insert. A definitive, easy-to-use guide to Southwestern reptiles! By Erik Stoops and Annette Wright.

6 x 9—128 pages . . . $9.95

TREASURES OF TIME

A user-friendly guide to ceramics found at Raven Site Ruins near Springerville, Arizona. Author/archaeologist James R. Cunkle catagorizes five of the primary groups of prehistoric ceramics and treats each in a separate chapter of in-depth information. Includes 24 page color insert.

6 x 9 — 216 Pages . . . $14.95

ARIZONA COOK BOOK

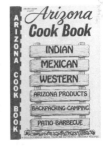

A taste of the Old Southwest! Sizzling Indian fry bread, prickly pear marmalade, sourdough biscuits, refried beans, beef jerky and cactus candy. By Al and Mildred Fischer. More than 250,000 copies in print!

5 1/2 x 8 1/2—144 Pages . . . $5.95

CHILI-LOVERS' COOK BOOK

Chili cookoff prize-winning recipes and regional favorites! The best of chili cookery, from mild to fiery, with and without beans. Plus a variety of taste-tempting foods made with chile peppers. 150,000 copies in print! By Al and Mildred Fischer.

5 1/2 x 8 1/2—128 pages . . . $5.95

More Outdoor Books from Golden West!

FISHING ARIZONA

Noted outdoors writer G. J. Sagi takes you fishing on 50 of Arizona's most popular lakes and streams revealing when, where and how to catch those lunkers!

5 1/2 x 8 1/2 — 152 Pages . . . $7.95

HORSE TRAILS IN ARIZONA

Complete guide to over 100 of Arizona's most beautiful equestrian trails, from the desert to the high country. Maps, directions to trailheads, water availability and more to ensure an unmatched experience for all who love hoseback riding. Lodging and "hitchin' post" restaurant information, too!

5 1/2 x 8 1/2 — 160 Pages . . . $9.95

ARIZONA OUTDOOR GUIDE

Guide to plants, animals, birds, rocks, minerals, geologic history, natural environments, landforms, resources, national forests and outdoor survival. Maps, photos, drawings, charts, index. *Arizona Outdoor Guide* by Ernest E. Snyder

5 1/2 x 8 1/2—128 pages. . . $6.95

HUNTING SMALL GAME IN ARIZONA

A complete guide for hunters and outdoorsmen. Information on all of Arizona's small game species plus turkey and javelina. Contains maps, weapons advice, animal characteristics, safety, first aid and clothing tips. By G. J. Sagi

5 1/2 x 8 1/2 — 144 Pages . . . $7.95

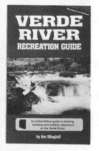

VERDE RIVER RECREATION GUIDE

Guide to Arizona's Verde River and its tributaries, section by section. For boaters, campers, hikers, tubers, naturalists. Includes types of water to be encountered, surrounding terrain, wildlife. Plus camping and boating advice, whitewater ratings, maps, photos, index. *Verde River Recreation Guide* by Jim Slingluff.

5 1/2 x 8 1/2—176 pages . . . $6.95

ORDER BLANK

GOLDEN WEST PUBLISHERS

☼ 4113 N. Longview Ave. • Phoenix, AZ 85014

602-265-4392 • **1-800-658-5830** • FAX 602-279-6901

Qty	Title	Price	Amount
	Arizona Adventure	6.95	
	Arizona Cook Book	5.95	
	Arizona Museums	9.95	
	Arizona Outdoor Guide	6.95	
	Cactus Country	6.95	
	Chili-Lovers' Cook Book	5.95	
	Discover Arizona!	6.95	
	Explore Arizona!	6.95	
	Fishing Arizona	7.95	
	Ghost Towns in Arizona	6.95	
	Hiking Arizona	6.95	
	Hiking Arizona II	6.95	
	Horse Trails in Arizona	9.95	
	Hunting Small Game in Arizona	7.95	
	Motorcycle Arizona!	9.95	
	Quest for the Dutchman's Gold	6.95	
	Snakes and other Reptiles of the SW	9.95	
	Talking Pots	19.95	
	Treasures of Time	14.95	
	Verde River Recreation Guide	6.95	
Add $2.00 to total order for shipping & handling			$2.00

☐ My Check or Money Order Enclosed. . . . . $ _____

☐ MasterCard   ☐ VISA

Acct. No.   Exp. Date

Signature

Name   Telephone

Address

City/State/Zip   **Call for FREE catalog**

9/94   MasterCard and VISA Orders Accepted ($20 Minimum)

Motorcycle

This order blank may be photo-copied.